Business Brilliance in Early Islam

"Commerce & Conviction: The Business Ventures of the Sahaba"

As I reflect on the purpose behind writing this book, I am filled with a deep sense of conviction and passion to influence the youth positively. Exploring the Sahaba's business life is not merely an academic pursuit but a heartfelt endeavor to impart valuable lessons and insights that can empower and inspire the next generation.

In today's fast-paced and interconnected world, where materialism and consumerism often overshadow spiritual values, it's more crucial than ever to remind our youth of the timeless wisdom and exemplary conduct exhibited by the Sahaba. Their commitment to Islam was not confined to the mosque or the battlefield but permeated every aspect of their lives, including their business endeavors.

As I delve into the wealth of knowledge and wisdom preserved in the books and historical accounts of the Sahaba, I am humbled by the depth and richness of their experiences. From the entrepreneurial spirit of Uthman ibn Affan to the philanthropy of Abdur-Rahman ibn Awf, each Sahabi exemplifies a unique facet of Islamic business ethics and values.

Through this book, I hope to offer a glimpse into the profound insights and practical lessons embedded in the business life of the Sahaba. It is not merely a historical narrative but a living testament to the enduring relevance of Islamic principles in commerce and trade.

My feelings are driven by a sincere desire to bridge the gap between tradition and modernity, offering the youth a roadmap for navigating the complexities of the contemporary business world while remaining rooted in faith and ethical conduct. I believe that by understanding and emulating the example the Sahaba sets, our youth can cultivate a sense of purpose, integrity, and responsibility in their entrepreneurial endeavors.

This book is more than just an overview; it is a call to action, a reminder of the transformative power of faith and the timeless wisdom of our Islamic heritage. Through its pages, I hope to instil in the hearts of the youth a renewed sense of pride in their identity as Muslims and a commitment to upholding the values of honesty, compassion, and social responsibility in all aspects of their lives.

In writing this book, I am fueled by a profound sense of duty and gratitude to Allah for blessing us with the guidance of the Quran and the example of the Prophet Muhammad (ﷺ), peace be upon him, and his noble companions. May this humble effort serve as a beacon of light for generations to come, illuminating the path of righteousness and prosperity in both this world and the Hereafter.

The belief of Ahl-us-Sunnah wal-Jamā'ah regarding the Companions

From the boundless mercy and kindness of Allah to His servants, and from His immense favor upon them, is His sending of a Messenger from among themselves. This Messenger was tasked with conveying the divine Message from their Lord, guiding them towards all that is beneficial, and warning them against all that may harm them.

Truly, the Prophet Muhammad (peace be upon him) fulfilled his duty of conveying this Message most completely and perfectly. He directed his Ummah, his community, towards every good deed and warned them against every evil.

Allah chose the best of this nation, the best of all nations, to accompany His Prophet and to learn from him. He honored them with the opportunity to witness the Prophet's noble character and to hear his teachings directly from his blessed lips. This is a bounty bestowed by Allah upon whomever He wills, and indeed, Allah possesses the greatest of bounties.

The Companions of the Prophet conveyed the guidance from Allah's Messenger in the most complete and perfect form. They will be rewarded greatly for their companionship with the Prophet, their participation in Jihad alongside him, and their noble efforts in spreading the message of Islam.

Furthermore, they will amass rewards from those who come after them, as they served as the bridge between them and the Messenger of Allah (peace be upon him). This is in accordance with his saying:
"Whoever calls for guidance, he will have a reward equal to the reward earned by those who practice that 4 guidance after him, and it will not reduce anything from their reward."

This hadith has been narrated by Muslim in his Sahih collection. Allah praised the Companions in His Mighty Book, and the Messenger of Allah (peace be upon him) praised them in his purified Sunnah. This alone suffices as a virtue and honor for them.

Allah says:
"And the foremost to embrace Islâm of the Muhâjirîn and the Ansâr and also those who followed them in goodness, Allâh is pleased with them and they are pleased with Him. Allâh has prepared for them gardens under which rivers flow (Paradise) to dwell therein forever. That is the supreme success." [Sûrah At-Tawbah: 100]

The Prophet () said: "The best of mankind is my generation, then those that come after them, then those that come after them." *Sahîh Hadîth: Reported by Al-Bukhârî and Muslim from the hadîth of Ibn Mas'ûd. Many*

Companions narrated this hadîth, amongst them 'Imrân Ibn Husayn and An-Nu'mân Ibn Bashîr. See As-Sahîhah of Imâm Al-Albânî: (699- 700).

The Prophet's Path of Commerce: Exploring the Role of Trade in the Life of Muhammad (ﷺ) (PBUH)

Before embarking on his prophetic mission, Muhammad (ﷺ)(PBUH) walked the dusty paths of trade, building not just a fortune but also a reputation for honesty, integrity, and shrewd business acumen. This experience profoundly shaped his character, leadership style, and ultimately, the nascent Islamic community's economic outlook. To truly understand the Prophet's life and legacy, we must delve into the world of commerce and its multifaceted impact on his journey.

From Caravans to Character: Early Life and Apprenticeship

Born into a family with ties to trade, Muhammad (ﷺ) (PBUH) began accompanying his uncles on merchant caravans at a young age. These journeys across the Arabian Peninsula not only fostered his understanding of geography and diverse cultures but also instilled in him valuable skills like negotiation, risk management, and financial responsibility.

He developed a reputation for fair dealing and trustworthiness, earning the nickname "al-Sadiq" – the truthful – a testament to his integrity. This reputation proved invaluable later, attracting followers who admired his moral character and leadership qualities honed through years of navigating the complex world of commerce.

Khadija's Partnership: A Flourishing Union of Love and Business

At the age of 25, Muhammad (ﷺ) (PBUH) entered into a business partnership with Khadija bint Khuwaylid, a successful and well-respected merchant. This union transcended mere commerce, blossoming into a loving marriage built on mutual respect and admiration. Khadija was impressed by Muhammad's (PBUH) honesty and business acumen, entrusting him with the leadership of her caravans.

Through this partnership, Muhammad (ﷺ)(PBUH) further honed his business skills, managing large trading expeditions and expanding Khadija's enterprise. This period not only provided financial stability but also offered invaluable lessons in leadership, delegation, and navigating challenging economic situations.

From Marketplace to Revelation: Trade's Influence on the Quran

The very environment of trade influenced the Quran's content and language. Terms like "barakah" (blessing), "riba" (usury), and "zakat" (obligatory charity) all stemmed from the commercial world, reflecting the importance of ethics, social responsibility, and fair dealing in economic transactions. The Quran emphasized just weights and measures, fair contracts, and compassion towards debtors, highlighting the values that guided Muhammad (ﷺ)(PBUH) own business practices.

Building an Islamic Economy: From Makkah to Madinah

When persecution forced the Prophet (PBUH) and his followers to migrate to Madinah, establishing a new community presented several challenges, including building a sustainable economy. Drawing upon his commercial experience, he laid the foundation for an Islamic economic system based on fairness, justice, and social responsibility.

He encouraged trade while advocating against exploitation and usury. The concept of "riba" was strictly prohibited, promoting ethical lending practices and protecting vulnerable individuals. Zakat, the obligatory charity, ensured wealth distribution and social welfare, fostering inclusivity and a sense of community.

Trade as a Means for Expansion: Spreading Islam beyond Borders

Trade routes served as arteries for not only goods but also for the dissemination of Islam. Muslim merchants, acting as ambassadors of faith, carried the message of Islam across vast distances. Their interactions with diverse communities sparked curiosity and dialogue, contributing to the peaceful expansion of the religion.

Muhammad (ﷺ)(PBUH) encouraged trade with non-Muslims, emphasizing respectful interactions and fair dealing. This approach built trust and fostered peaceful relations, demonstrating Islam's compatibility with commerce and its potential as a bridge between cultures.

Beyond Profit: Trade as a Tool for Social Upliftment

The Prophet (PBUH) did not view trade solely as a means for personal gain but also as a tool for social upliftment. He encouraged employment opportunities through trade, empowering individuals and alleviating poverty. He promoted small businesses and supported women's participation in commerce, challenging traditional gender roles and fostering economic independence.

Trade also facilitated the construction of essential infrastructure like wells and marketplaces, benefiting the entire community. The Prophet (PBUH) advocated for ethical pricing and condemned hoarding, ensuring essential goods remained accessible to all.

A Legacy of Ethics and Empowerment: The Enduring Impact

The Prophet's (PBUH) involvement in trade left an enduring legacy on Islamic economic thought and practice.

His emphasis on ethical conduct, social responsibility, and fair dealing continues to shape Muslim business practices worldwide. His approach to trade fostered inclusivity, empowered individuals, and contributed to the economic stability and flourishing of the early Islamic community.

Beyond Profits: Exploring the Unwritten Legacy

While historical records document the Prophet's (PBUH) business acumen and economic contributions, his personal relationship with wealth and trade holds deeper meaning. His simple lifestyle, devoid of extravagance, and his generosity towards the less fortunate serve as powerful ethical guides

The Moral Compass of Trade: Exploring Ethics and Principles of Islamic Commerce Across the bustling marketplaces and sprawling trade routes of early Islam, commerce wasn't merely a pursuit of profit; it was woven into the fabric of faith, guided by a distinct set of ethical principles. This essay delves into the rich tapestry of ethics and principles that shaped Islamic commerce, exploring how they aimed to create a just, equitable, and responsible system of trade, leaving a lasting legacy that continues to resonate today.

Rooted in Revelation: Divine Guidance for Ethical Conduct

The foundation of Islamic ethics in commerce lies in the Quran and the teachings of Prophet Muhammad (ﷺ)(PBUH). The Quran emphasizes fairness, honesty, and compassion in all aspects of life, including economic transactions. Verses like "Woe to those who defraud [in measuring and weighing]" (Al-Mutaffifin: 1-3) and "And do not consume one another's wealth unjustly through fraud" (Al-Baqarah: 188) serve as stern admonitions against unethical practices.

Prophet Muhammad (ﷺ)(PBUH) further exemplified these principles through his personal conduct and teachings. His reputation for honesty and fair dealing earned him the nickname "al-Sadiq" (the truthful). He advocated for just weights and measures, condemned hoarding and exploitation, and encouraged generosity towards the less fortunate.

Pillars of Ethical Trade: Justice, Transparency, and Social Responsibility

Built upon this divine foundation, several core principles guided Islamic commerce:

Justice and Fairness: This encompassed fair pricing, avoiding deception, and adhering to agreed-upon contracts. The concept of "adl" (justice) formed the cornerstone of economic interactions, ensuring a level playing field for all participants.

Transparency and Honesty: Concealing information, using misleading statements, or engaging in fraudulent practices were strictly prohibited. The emphasis on "sidq" (truthfulness) encouraged transparency in all market dealings.

Social Responsibility: Wealth wasn't seen as an individual accumulation but as a means for collective well-being. The principle of "zakat" (obligatory charity) ensured wealth distribution and social welfare, while "waqf" endowments supported public works and charitable institutions.
Prohibitive Measures: Curbing Exploitation and Greed

Beyond positive principles, clear prohibitions safeguarded ethical conduct:

In Islamic commerce, the ethical dimension holds paramount importance. Central to this ethical framework are prohibitive measures aimed at curbing exploitation and greed. Islam emphasizes fair and just economic practices that prioritize the well-being of individuals and society over excessive profit-seeking. This essay delves into the prohibitive measures prescribed by Islamic principles to regulate commerce, mitigate exploitation, and foster a more equitable economic system.

Prohibition of Riba (Interest):
At the core of Islamic commerce is the prohibition of riba, or interest-based transactions. Riba is considered exploitative as it generates wealth without productive effort and can lead to economic inequality. Islamic law categorically prohibits any form of interest, emphasizing instead equitable transactions where profit is tied to risk-taking and productive contribution.

Prohibition of Gharar (Uncertainty) and Maisir (Gambling):

Islamic commerce also prohibits transactions involving excessive uncertainty (gharar) and gambling (maisir). These practices are seen as exploitative and detrimental to economic stability. By prohibiting such transactions, Islam aims to ensure clarity, transparency, and fairness in all commercial dealings.

Ethical Business Conduct:
Islamic commerce emphasizes ethical business conduct rooted in principles of honesty, integrity, and trustworthiness. Business owners are encouraged to fulfill their contractual obligations, honor agreements, and uphold the highest ethical standards in their interactions with customers, suppliers, and stakeholders.

Social Responsibility:
Islam underscores the concept of social responsibility in commerce, whereby businesses are encouraged to consider the broader societal impact of their actions. This includes fair treatment of employees, environmental stewardship, and giving back to the community through charitable initiatives and welfare programs.

Prohibition of Exploitative Practices:
Islamic principles prohibit exploitative practices such as hoarding, price manipulation, and monopolistic behavior. These practices are seen as antithetical to the principles of justice and fairness in commerce. Instead, Islam advocates for free and open markets where competition is encouraged, and fair pricing prevails.

Protection of Consumer Rights:
Islamic commerce places a strong emphasis on protecting consumer rights. Businesses are obligated to provide goods and services that meet quality standards, fulfill contractual obligations, and refrain from deceptive practices. Consumers have the right to fair treatment, accurate information, and recourse in case of disputes.

Wealth Redistribution:
Islamic commerce advocates for wealth redistribution through mechanisms such as zakat (obligatory almsgiving) and sadaqah (voluntary charity). These practices aim to alleviate poverty, reduce inequality, and ensure that wealth is circulated within society rather than concentrated in the hands of a few.

Legal Framework:

Islamic jurisprudence provides a comprehensive legal framework governing commercial transactions. This includes guidelines on contracts, partnerships, sales, and other aspects of commerce. The objective is to ensure that transactions are conducted in accordance with Islamic principles and that disputes are resolved fairly and justly.

Guilds and Regulations: Ensuring Ethical Practices on the Ground

To translate these principles into action, communities formed guilds for various crafts and professions. These guilds established standards for quality, pricing, and ethical conduct, fostering trust and transparency within the marketplace. Additionally, caliphs promulgated regulations addressing issues like weights and measures, contracts, and dispute resolution, creating a stable and predictable environment for ethical commerce.

Beyond Borders: Spreading Ethical Commerce Through Trade Routes

Muslim merchants didn't just adhere to these principles themselves; they acted as ambassadors of ethical conduct on trade routes across the world. Their reputation for fairness and integrity helped break down stereotypes and establish trust with diverse communities. This dissemination of ethical values contributed to the positive image of Islam and influenced global trade practices in the long run.

Challenges and Adaptations: Navigating a Dynamic World

Maintaining ethical practices wasn't always easy. Political instability, competition, and evolving market dynamics presented complex challenges. However, Islamic scholars and jurists continually adapted and interpreted economic principles to address new situations. This adaptability ensured the ongoing relevance of ethical guidelines and prevented rigid interpretations from hindering economic progress.

Legacy and Relevance: A Compass for Modern Times

The principles of Islamic commerce continue to hold relevance in today's globalized world. Concepts like fair trade, responsible investment, and social responsibility resonate with contemporary concerns about sustainable development and ethical capitalism. Studying these principles offers valuable insights into creating a more just and equitable economic system for all.

The Legacy and Influence: How the Sahaba Shaped Islamic Trade Practices

The Sahaba, companions of Prophet Muhammad (ﷺ)(PBUH), played a pivotal role in shaping the early Islamic community, including establishing and influencing its unique approach to trade. Beyond mere merchants, they served as exemplars, administrators, and innovators, leaving an enduring legacy on Islamic commerce that continues to resonate today.

Setting the Standard: Exemplary Conduct and Leadership

The Sahaba witnessed and adhered to Prophet Muhammad's (PBUH) own ethical approach to trade. They observed his emphasis on honesty, fairness, and social responsibility, translating these principles into their own business practices. Their actions served as a model for future generations, establishing a benchmark for ethical conduct within the Islamic world.

Administration and Regulation: Laying the Foundation for a Just System

Beyond personal conduct, the Sahaba took on administrative roles, shaping the legal and regulatory framework governing trade. Caliphs like Umar ibn al-Khattab established regulations on weights and measures, standardized coinage, and ensured fair market practices. These initiatives fostered trust and transparency within the marketplace, laying the foundation for a stable and just economic system.

Adapting to Challenges: Innovative Solutions for a Growing Community

As the Islamic community expanded, new challenges arose in the realm of trade. The Sahaba, known for their adaptability and resourcefulness, devised innovative solutions. For instance, they developed the "hawala" system, an early form of money transfer, facilitating secure cross-border transactions. This innovation addressed the need for secure financial instruments in a growing empire.

Disseminating Knowledge: Sharing Best Practices and Ethical Guidelines

The Sahaba actively transmitted their knowledge and experiences to subsequent generations. They documented principles of Islamic commerce, shared narratives of ethical dilemmas and their resolutions, and engaged in scholarly discussions on emerging challenges. This transmission of knowledge ensured the continuity of ethical practices and facilitated their adaptation to evolving circumstances.

Beyond Commercial Activity: Social Responsibility and Philanthropy

The Sahaba understood that wealth wasn't just for personal gain; it was a tool for social good. They actively engaged in philanthropy, utilizing their wealth to support the less fortunate, fund public works, and establish educational institutions. Their commitment to social responsibility became a hallmark of Islamic commerce, shaping its impact on communities beyond simply material exchanges.

Lasting Influence: Shaping Ethics and Practices over Centuries

The legacy of the Sahaba in shaping Islamic trade practices extends far beyond their immediate era. Their emphasis on ethical conduct, social responsibility, and innovation continues to influence Muslim merchants and scholars worldwide. Their contributions helped shape Islamic economic thought, legal frameworks, and business practices, leaving a lasting mark on the world of commerce.

Examining Individual Impacts: Exploring Specific Contributions

While examining the collective impact of the Sahaba, it's important to acknowledge the diversity of their experiences and contributions. Exploring the individual roles of figures like Abd al-Rahman ibn Awf, Khadija bint Khuwaylid, and Zayd ibn Thabit offers a deeper understanding of how specific individuals translated principles into tangible practices and addressed pressing challenges of their time.

Continuing Relevance: Lessons for Contemporary Practices

In an increasingly globalized world, studying the ethical framework established by the Sahaba offers valuable insights for contemporary challenges. Concepts like fair trade, responsible investment, and social responsibility remain relevant concerns. Exploring the historical application of these principles can inform discussions and inspire the development of more ethical and sustainable practices in today's world.

بِسْمِ اللّٰهِ الرَّحْمٰنِ الرَّحِيم

الَّذِينَ يَأْكُلُونَ الرِّبَوٰا لَا يَقُومُونَ إِلَّا كَمَا يَقُومُ الَّذِى يَتَخَبَّطُهُ الشَّيْطَانُ مِنَ الْمَسِّ ذَٰلِكَ بِأَنَّهُمْ قَالُوٓا إِنَّمَا الْبَيْعُ مِثْلُ الرِّبَوٰا وَأَحَلَّ اللّٰهُ الْبَيْعَ وَحَرَّمَ الرِّبَوٰا فَمَن جَآءَهُ مَوْعِظَةٌ مِّن رَّبِّهِ فَانتَهَىٰ فَلَهُ مَا سَلَفَ وَأَمْرُهُ إِلَى اللّٰهِ وَمَنْ عَادَ فَأُولَٰٓئِكَ أَصْحَٰبُ النَّارِ هُمْ فِيهَا خَٰلِدُونَ ٢٧٥

وہ جو سود کھاتے ہیں قیامت کے دن نہ کھڑے ہوں گے مگر جیسے کھڑا ہوتا ہے وہ جسے آسیب نے چھو کر مخبوط بنادیا ہو یہ اس لئے کہ انہوں نے کہا بیع بھی تو سود ہی کے مانند ہے اور اللہ نے حلال کیا بیع اور

حرام کیا سود تو جسے اس کے رب کے پاس سے نصیحت آئی اور وہ باز
رہا تو اسے حلال ہے جو پہلے لے چکا اور اس کا کام خدا کے سپرد ہے
اور جو اب ایسی حرکت کرے گا تو وہ دوزخی ہے وہ اس میں مدتوں رہیں
گے۔

SURAH AL-BAQARAH AYAT 275 (2:275 QURAN)

Those who consume interest will stand ☐on Judgment
Day☐ like those driven to madness by Satan's touch. That
is because they say, "Trade is no different than interest."
But Allah has permitted trading and forbidden interest.
Whoever refrains—after having received warning from
their Lord—may keep their previous gains, and their case is
left to Allah. As for those who persist, it is they who will be
the residents of the Fire. They will be there forever.

یٰۤاَیُّهَا الَّذِیْنَ اٰمَنُوْا لَا تَاْكُلُوْۤا اَمْوَالَكُمْ بَیْنَكُمْ بِالْبَاطِلِ اِلَّاۤ اَنْ
تَكُوْنَ تِجَارَةً عَنْ تَرَاضٍ مِّنْكُمْ۔ وَ لَا تَقْتُلُوْۤا اَنْفُسَكُمْ ☐-اِنَّ
(29)اللّٰهَ كَانَ بِكُمْ رَحِیْمًا

اے ایمان والو! باطل طریقے سے آپس میں ایک دوسرے کے مال نہ کھاؤ
البتہ یہ (ہو) کہ تمہاری باہمی رضامندی سے تجارت ہو اور اپنی جانوں کو
قتل نہ کرو۔ بیشک اللہ تم پر مہربان ہے۔

O believers! Do not devour one another's wealth illegally,
but rather trade by mutual consent. And do not kill ☐each
other or☐ yourselves. Surely Allah is ever Merciful to you.
Surah An Nisa Ayat 29

Brief overview of the importance of trade in the early Islamic community.

The Caravans of Faith: Exploring Business and Trade in the Early Islamic Era

The rise of Islam in the 7th century CE marked a momentous shift in the global landscape. From the arid sands of Arabia, a new faith emerged, destined to shape not only religious beliefs but also economic and social trajectories across vast regions. Fueling this rapid expansion was a potent force: business and trade. This essay delves into the intricate tapestry of business practices and commercial activities that intertwined with the early Islamic community, highlighting their multifaceted impact and lasting legacy.

Pre-Islamic Arabia: Laying the Groundwork for Commercial Enterprise

Prior to the advent of Islam, the Arabian Peninsula wasn't a major economic hub. However, its strategic location served as a vital transit point for established trade routes connecting the East and West. Spices, silks, and other valuable commodities flowed through caravan networks like the frankincense and spice routes, enriching kingdoms like Saba and Nabataea. This exposure to commerce influenced early Arab society, fostering a spirit of entrepreneurship and an understanding of international trade dynamics.

Prophet Muhammad (ﷺ) and the Seeds of a Prosperous Community:

Prophet Muhammad (ﷺ) (PBUH), himself a merchant before his prophethood, recognized the importance of trade for the nascent Muslim community. His wife, Khadija bint Khuwaylid, was a highly successful businesswoman, managing caravans and demonstrating the economic potential of commerce. Their example encouraged other Muslims to engage in trade, contributing to the early community's financial stability and growth.

Beyond Individual Success: Trade's Economic Engine:

Trade not only benefited individual merchants but also served as a crucial economic engine for the community. Wealth generated through commercial activities financed infrastructure development, social welfare programs, and military campaigns. Figures like Abd al-Rahman ibn Awf, known for his astute financial management, served as treasurers, ensuring the judicious utilization of these resources.

Furthermore, trade diversified the community's economy, traditionally reliant on agriculture. Essential goods and resources became accessible through trade routes, ensuring food security and providing materials crucial for daily life. Additionally, caravan creation fueled job creation, offering employment opportunities and promoting economic activity beyond traditional sectors. This diversification not only strengthened the overall economy but also facilitated social mobility through avenues of commercial success.

Breaking Barriers and Empowering Communities:

The rigid tribal hierarchies of pre-Islamic Arabia were challenged by the dynamic world of trade. Individuals who excelled in commercial endeavors, regardless of their social background, gained recognition and wealth, disrupting established hierarchies. This meritocratic aspect of trade attracted diverse talents from various tribes, fostering inclusivity and breaking down social barriers within the community.

Moreover, trade empowered women by creating opportunities for them to participate actively in economic activities. Merchants like Khadija and Shifa bint Abdullah defied traditional gender roles by demonstrating exceptional entrepreneurial spirit and leadership. Their success paved the way for greater female participation in trade, challenging societal norms and contributing to the economic empowerment of women.

Beyond Borders: Trade as a Bridge for Diplomacy and Faith:

Trade routes transcended the realm of mere goods and services, evolving into conduits for cultural exchange and diplomatic interactions. Merchants served as cultural ambassadors, fostering understanding and peaceful coexistence with neighboring civilizations. Through interactions with diverse populations, they transmitted knowledge, languages, and customs, enriching the lives of both communities.

Furthermore, trade routes became crucial channels for the dissemination of Islamic teachings. As merchants ventured across vast distances, they shared their faith with individuals from different backgrounds, contributing significantly to the expansion of the Islamic world. This peaceful propagation of faith through trade helped establish Islam as a major religious force, transcending geographical boundaries and fostering religious solidarity across diverse populations.

Strengthening the Internal Fabric: Trade and the Pillars of Islam:

The wealth generated through trade fueled the Islamic community's commitment to its core values. The principle of Zakat, an obligatory charity for the underprivileged, ensured the equitable distribution of wealth and fostered social cohesion within the community. This commitment to social justice and care for the less fortunate resonated deeply with the teachings of Islam and further strengthened the internal fabric of the community.

Additionally, trade routes facilitated the smooth flow of pilgrims to Mecca, the holiest site in Islam. This annual pilgrimage served as a powerful unifying force, bringing together Muslims from diverse regions and backgrounds.

Trade routes facilitated their travel, allowing them to participate in this central ritual and experience the cultural exchange and religious solidarity that pilgrimage fostered.

Ethical Compass and a Commitment to Knowledge:

Islamic economic principles played a crucial role in regulating trade and instilling ethical values within the community. The concepts of just pricing, fair dealing, and the prohibition of usury (riba) ensured that commerce operated within a framework of ethical conduct. This commitment to ethical principles not only fostered trust and transparency within the community but also distinguished Muslim merchants from their contemporaries, adding to their reputation for fairness and integrity.

Introduction to the concept of Sahaba and their significance in Islam.

The Companions of the Prophet: A Beacon of Guidance and Inspiration

Within the tapestry of Islamic history, the lives and characters of the Sahaba, the companions of Prophet Muhammad (ﷺ)(PBUH), occupy a central and irreplaceable position. More than just individuals who witnessed his revelation, they embodied the first generation of Muslims who translated his teachings into a living, breathing society. Their significance extends far beyond mere historical interest, for they serve as enduring sources of guidance, inspiration, and understanding for Muslims across generations.

Defining the Sahaba: The term "Sahaba" in Arabic refers to "companions" or "friends." Traditionally, the definition encompasses those who met Prophet Muhammad (ﷺ)in person, believed in him while he was alive, and died as Muslims. This broad definition encompasses a diverse group of individuals, ranging from the earliest converts like Khadija, his wife, and Abu Bakr, his closest friend, to later converts like Khalid ibn al-Walid, a formidable military leader.

Their Significance: The Sahaba held immense religious and historical significance for several reasons:

Transmitters of Knowledge: They served as the primary custodians and transmitters of the Prophet's teachings, both religious and practical. They memorized his words, actions, and rulings, forming the basis for the vast corpus of Islamic knowledge known as Hadith. Their firsthand accounts ensured the authenticity and accurate transmission of Prophet Muhammad's legacy.

Exemplars of Faith: Their lives exemplified the practical application of Islamic principles in daily life. They faced persecution, endured hardships, and fought battles, all while remaining steadfast in their faith. Their commitment to Islam and unwavering loyalty to the Prophet served as a model for generations of Muslims to emulate.

Founders of Institutions: The Sahaba played a crucial role in establishing foundational Islamic institutions and practices. They participated in setting up the first Islamic community in Medina, shaping its social, political, and economic structures. Their contributions laid the groundwork for the development of Islamic jurisprudence, education, and social welfare systems.

Sources of Diversity: The Sahaba were a diverse group, representing different tribes, social backgrounds, and personalities. This diversity allowed for a richness of perspectives and contributed to the dynamism of early Islamic society. Their varied experiences offered insights into adapting the message of Islam to different contexts and needs.

Continuing Inspiration: Their stories continue to inspire and motivate Muslims worldwide. Their struggles, triumphs, and unwavering faith serve as a reminder of the power of conviction and the importance of upholding Islamic values. Studying their lives allows Muslims to connect with the roots of their faith and gain a deeper understanding of its principles.

Categories of Sahaba: It's important to acknowledge that not all Sahaba were equal in their closeness to the Prophet or the role they played in shaping Islam. Some key categories emerged:

The Ten Promised Paradise: A group of ten companions specifically mentioned by the Prophet as guaranteed

Paradise. They served as advisors, leaders, and role models for the wider community.

Mujahidun: Those who participated in military campaigns alongside the Prophet, defending the nascent Muslim community. Their bravery and sacrifice laid the foundation for the expansion of Islam.

Ansar and Muhajirun: The Ansar were the residents of Medina who welcomed the Prophet and his followers (Muhajirun) who migrated from Mecca. Their hospitality and support were crucial for the survival and growth of the early Muslim community.

Scholars and Jurists: Individuals who became renowned for their knowledge of Islamic law and interpretations of the Quran and Hadith. Their rulings and scholarship formed the basis for Islamic legal and theological schools of thought.

Women: Although often overlooked, women Sahaba played crucial roles in social, economic, and religious spheres. They participated in battles, provided medical care, taught Quran, and managed community affairs. They offered unique perspectives and experiences that enriched the development of Islamic society.

Studying the Sahaba: Engaging with the lives and achievements of the Sahaba can be a valuable pursuit for Muslims and non-Muslims alike. Here are some approaches:

Reading Biographies: Numerous biographies delve deep into the lives of individual Sahaba, offering insights into their personalities, challenges, and contributions.

Exploring Hadith Collections: Reading Hadith collections allows for direct access to the sayings and actions of the Sahaba, providing practical lessons and glimpses into their interactions with the Prophet.

Historical Narratives: Studying historical accounts of the early Islamic period paints a broader picture of the social and political context in which the Sahaba lived, allowing for a more nuanced understanding of their actions.

Critical Analysis: While respecting their revered status, engaging in critical analysis of their lives and decisions allows for a deeper and more objective understanding of their historical and religious significance.

The Sahaba occupy a unique and important space in the Islamic tradition. Their lives and legacy hold

Narrated 'Abdullah bin Mughaffal:

that the Messenger of Allah (ﷺ) said: "(Fear) Allah! (Fear) Allah regarding my Companions! Do not make them objects of insults after me. Whoever loves them, it is out of love of me that he loves them. And whoever hates them, it is out of hatred for me that he hates them. And whoever harms them, he has harmed me, and whoever harms me, he has offended Allah, and whoever offends Allah, [then] he shall soon be punished."

Narrated 'Abdullah bin Mughaffal:

that the Messenger of Allah (ﷺ) said: "(Fear) Allah! (Fear) Allah regarding my Companions! Do not make them objects of insults after me. Whoever loves them, it is out of love of me that he loves them. And whoever hates them, it is out of hatred for me that he hates them. And whoever harms them, he has harmed me, and whoever harms me, he has offended Allah, and whoever offends Allah, [then] he shall soon be punished."

حَدَّثَنَا مُحَمَّدُ بْنُ يَحْيَى، قَالَ حَدَّثَنَا يَعْقُوبُ بْنُ إِبْرَاهِيمَ بْنِ سَعْدٍ، قَالَ حَدَّثَنَا عَبِيدَةُ ابْنُ أَبِي رَائِطَةَ، عَنْ عَبْدِ الرَّحْمَنِ بْنِ زِيَادٍ، عَنْ عَبْدِ اللَّهِ بْنِ مُغَفَّلٍ، قَالَ قَالَ رَسُولُ اللَّهِ صلى الله عليه وسلم " اللَّهَ اللَّهَ فِي أَصْحَابِي اللَّهَ اللَّهَ فِي أَصْحَابِي لاَ تَتَّخِذُوهُمْ غَرَضًا بَعْدِي فَمَنْ أَحَبَّهُمْ فَبِحُبِّي أَحَبَّهُمْ وَمَنْ أَبْغَضَهُمْ فَبِبُغْضِي أَبْغَضَهُمْ وَمَنْ آذَاهُمْ فَقَدْ آذَانِي وَمَنْ آذَانِي فَقَدْ آذَى اللَّهَ وَمَنْ آذَى اللَّهَ فَيُوشِكُ أَنْ يَأْخُذَهُ " . قَالَ أَبُو عِيسَى هَذَا حَدِيثٌ حَسَنٌ غَرِيبٌ لاَ نَعْرِفُهُ إِلاَّ مِنْ هَذَا الْوَجْهِ

(Sunan Tirmidhi, Hadith: 3862 and Sahih Ibn Hibban; Al Ihsan, Hadith: 7256)
This Hadith has been declared sound (hasan gharib) by Imam Tirmidhi (rahimahullah) and authentic (sahih) by Imam Ibn Hibban (rahimahullah).

The Ethical Business Practices and Philanthropic Legacy of Prophet Muhammad (ﷺ)(PBUH)

The business life of Prophet Muhammad (ﷺ)(peace be upon him) is a significant aspect of his biography, highlighting his integrity, honesty, and entrepreneurial spirit. Before receiving revelations and embarking on his prophetic mission, Muhammad (ﷺ)(peace be upon him) was involved in trade and commerce, gaining valuable experience and reputation as a trustworthy businessman. Here is an overview of Prophet Muhammad's (peace be upon him) business life:

Early Years in Trade:

Muhammad (ﷺ)(peace be upon him) grew up in Mecca, a city known for its bustling trade routes and markets. He gained exposure to business from an early age, accompanying his uncle Abu Talib on trading journeys to various regions in Arabia. Through these experiences, Muhammad (ﷺ)(peace be upon him) learned the intricacies of trade, including negotiation, pricing, and market dynamics.

Employment with Khadija:

One of the most significant phases of Muhammad's (peace be upon him) business life was his employment with Khadija bint Khuwaylid, a wealthy and successful businesswoman in Mecca. Khadija hired Muhammad (ﷺ)(peace be upon him) to manage her trade caravans, impressed by his honesty, integrity, and business acumen. Muhammad's (peace be upon him) successful management of Khadija's business operations earned him a reputation as Al-Amin, the trustworthy one.

Marriage to Khadija:

Muhammad's (peace be upon him) business relationship with Khadija eventually led to their marriage, marking the beginning of a prosperous partnership. As Khadija's husband, Muhammad (ﷺ)(peace be upon him) continued to oversee her trade ventures, expanding their commercial activities to include trading in goods such as textiles, spices, and luxury items. Their marriage was characterized by mutual respect, love, and cooperation in both personal and business matters.

Fair Trade Practices:

Throughout his business endeavors, Muhammad (ﷺ)(peace be upon him) adhered strictly to principles of fairness, honesty, and integrity. He was known for his scrupulous honesty in all his dealings, earning the trust and respect of his contemporaries. Muhammad's (peace be upon him) commitment to fair trade practices set a high standard for ethical conduct in business and served as a model for future generations of Muslims.

Philanthropy and Charity:

Despite his success in business, Muhammad (ﷺ)(peace be upon him) maintained a strong sense of social responsibility and compassion for the less fortunate. He was known for his generosity and philanthropy, using his wealth to support widows, orphans, and the poor in Mecca.

Muhammad's (peace be upon him) commitment to charity and social justice reflected his deep compassion for humanity and his adherence to the principles of Islam.

Legacy of Business Ethics:

The business practices of Prophet Muhammad (ﷺ)(peace be upon him) continue to serve as a source of inspiration for Muslims around the world. His emphasis on honesty, integrity, and fairness in trade laid the foundation for a strong tradition of ethical business conduct in Islam. Today, Muslims strive to emulate the example of Muhammad (ﷺ)(peace be upon him) in their professional lives, upholding his principles of honesty, fairness, and compassion in all their dealings.

In summary, Prophet Muhammad's (peace be upon him) business life exemplified principles of honesty, integrity, and compassion, serving as a model for ethical business conduct in Islam. His successful career in trade, coupled with his commitment to philanthropy and social justice, underscores the importance of ethical values in both personal and professional endeavors.

Abu Bakr al-Siddiq

The Life of Abu Bakr Siddiq: A Pillar of Islam and Legacy of Leadership

Early Life and Laying the Foundation for Success:

Born into a well-regarded Meccan family known for their textile trade, Abu Bakr developed a keen understanding of commerce from a young age. He honed his skills in negotiation, risk management, and building trust with diverse customers. His meticulous bookkeeping and reputation for honesty earned him the nickname "al-Siddiq," the truthful.

Beyond personal gain, Abu Bakr viewed trade as a means to support his community. He actively participated in caravans, fostering economic activity and forging valuable relationships across the Arabian Peninsula. His generosity and fair dealing built trust and respect, establishing him as a reliable and ethical merchant.

The Business Acumen of Abu Bakr Siddiq: Ethical Trade and Community Building
Before embracing Islam and becoming the first Caliph, Abu Bakr Siddiq established himself as a prominent and respected merchant in Mecca. His business acumen, characterized by ethical practices and a deep-rooted commitment to his community, offers valuable insights into the intersection of commerce and faith in early Islamic society.

Embracing Islam and Aligning Faith with Business:

Abu Bakr was among the first converts to Islam, drawn to Prophet Muhammad's (PBUH) message of social justice and compassion. He readily embraced the ethical principles outlined in the Quran, ensuring his business practices aligned with his newfound faith.

He championed fair pricing, avoided usury (riba), and treated customers and employees with respect. This ethical approach not only resonated with his values but also attracted new customers who appreciated his honesty and integrity.

Supporting the Prophet's Mission:

Abu Bakr's unwavering support for Prophet Muhammad (ﷺ)(PBUH) extended beyond the spiritual realm. He used his financial resources to support the early Muslim community, providing refuge for persecuted Muslims and funding crucial initiatives like the Hijrah, the migration to Madinah.

His financial backing played a pivotal role in establishing the first Islamic community in Madinah, showcasing how commerce could be harnessed for the greater good and aligned with religious values.

Beyond personal gain, Abu Bakr viewed trade as a means to support his community. He actively participated in caravans, fostering economic activity and forging valuable relationships across the Arabian Peninsula. His generosity and fair dealing built trust and respect, establishing him as a reliable and ethical merchant.

Before embracing Islam and becoming the first Caliph, Abu Bakr Siddiq established himself as a prominent and respected merchant in Mecca. His business acumen, characterized by ethical practices and a deep-rooted commitment to his community, offers valuable insights into the intersection of commerce and faith in early Islamic society.

Leadership during Challenging Times:

Following Prophet Muhammad's (PBUH) death, Abu Bakr assumed the caliphate at a critical juncture. Facing internal rebellions and external threats, his leadership skills and understanding of trade came into play.

He navigated these challenges with strategic use of economic resources, consolidating power by strategically allocating funds and mobilizing resources for military campaigns. This ability to leverage his business acumen for political stability served the nascent Islamic state well.

Beyond Politics: Community Building and Social Responsibility:

While his political leadership is well-documented, Abu Bakr's commitment to his community extended far beyond governance. He used his wealth to support the underprivileged, provide for families affected by conflict, and invest in public infrastructure projects.

He actively encouraged commerce within the community, promoting fair trade practices and fostering economic opportunities for marginalized groups. This focus on social responsibility embodied the Islamic principle of zakat (obligatory charity) and ensured prosperity was shared within the community.

Lessons from Abu Bakr's Business Legacy:

Abu Bakr's life offers valuable lessons for individuals and businesses seeking to integrate ethical principles into their commercial endeavors:

Integrity as the Foundation: His unwavering commitment to honesty and fair dealing serves as a reminder that ethical conduct is vital for building trust and long-term success.
Faith as a Guiding Force: Harmonizing business practices with religious values demonstrates how commerce can be a tool for positive social change and community building.
Community Responsibility: His focus on supporting the less fortunate and investing in public welfare highlights the importance of using business success to contribute to the greater good.
Strategic Use of Resources: His ability to leverage his financial acumen for political stability and community development showcases the power of wise resource management.

Beyond Historical Significance:

While rooted in a specific historical context, Abu Bakr's story holds relevance for contemporary businesses and individuals navigating the complexities of the modern world. His principles of ethical conduct, social responsibility, and community engagement offer valuable guidance for building sustainable and responsible business practices that contribute to a just and equitable society.

Further Exploration:

Examining specific examples of how Abu Bakr resolved ethical dilemmas encountered in his business dealings can provide practical insights for contemporary challenges.
Exploring the interpretations of his legacy by different Islamic scholars and thinkers can offer diverse perspectives on the application of his principles in various social and economic contexts.
Analyzing the potential for incorporating his values into modern business models and corporate social responsibility initiatives can spark meaningful dialogue and contribute to the development of more ethical and sustainable business practices in the globalized world.
By delving deeper into the business life of Abu Bakr Siddiq, we gain valuable insights into the intersection of faith, ethics, and community building in the realm of commerce. His legacy continues to inspire individuals and businesses, encouraging them to navigate the world of commerce with integrity, responsibility, and a focus on contributing to a better future

Uthman Ibn Affan: A Life Dedicated to Trade, Service, and Stewardship

Uthman ibn Affan (579-656 CE), the third Caliph of Islam, embodied the multifaceted role Muslims played in society, excelling not only as a religious and political leader but also as a shrewd and generous businessman. While his contributions in codifying the Quran and expanding the Islamic empire are widely acknowledged, delving deeper into his fascinating business life reveals a unique blend of acumen, ethical principles, and social responsibility that continues to inspire generations.

Early Life and Business Prowess:

Born into a wealthy Meccan family renowned for trade, Uthman inherited a strong business acumen. Unlike other prominent companions of Prophet Muhammad (ﷺ)(PBUH) who primarily traded within Arabia, Uthman ventured farther, establishing extensive trade networks across Syria, Persia, and East Africa. This exposure to diverse cultures and markets honed his business skills, making him a pioneer in international trade for the early Muslim community.

His success stemmed from several key principles:

Integrity and Ethical Conduct: Uthman upheld Islamic principles of fairness and honesty in all his dealings. He was known for his just pricing, transparency, and avoidance of exploitative practices, earning him the trust and respect of both Muslim and non-Muslim merchants.

Innovation and Risk Management: He wasn't afraid to explore new markets and implement innovative strategies. He diversified his investments, established partnerships with reliable individuals, and managed risks prudently, ensuring the sustainability of his ventures.

Philanthropy and Social Responsibility: Uthman's wealth wasn't just for personal gain. He actively engaged in philanthropy, supporting the less fortunate, funding public works, and sponsoring expeditions for the spread of Islam. This commitment to social responsibility resonated with his faith and solidified his reputation as a generous and compassionate leader.

Beyond Individual Success: Impact on the Early Muslim Community:

Uthman's business acumen went beyond his personal prosperity. He played a pivotal role in bolstering the economic well-being of the early Muslim community in several ways:

Financial Support for the Prophet's Mission: During the early years of Islam, facing persecution in Mecca, Uthman provided crucial financial support to Prophet Muhammad (ﷺ)(PBUH) and his followers, enabling them to survive and continue their mission.

Economic Integration and Expansion: By establishing trade links with diverse regions, Uthman introduced new goods and commodities, stimulating economic activity within the Muslim community and fostering integration with neighboring regions.

Job Creation and Skills Development: His vast trading network created numerous employment opportunities for Muslims, contributing to their economic empowerment and skill development.

A Legacy of Ethical Commerce and Responsible Leadership:

Uthman's life offers valuable lessons for aspiring entrepreneurs and leaders:

Ethical principles as the foundation of success: Just as Uthman's integrity and fair dealing formed the bedrock of his business success, modern entrepreneurs can cultivate trust and loyalty by adhering to ethical practices.

Innovation and social responsibility: By embracing responsible innovation and integrating social responsibility into business models, leaders can contribute to sustainable growth and positive societal impact.

Leadership through service: Uthman's commitment to the well-being of the community serves as a reminder that true leadership often lies in serving others and working for the greater good.

Beyond Business: Exploring the Multifaceted Leader:

While Uthman's business life holds valuable insights, understanding his full legacy requires exploring other aspects of his journey:

Contributions as Caliph: His role in codifying the Quran, expanding the Islamic empire, and promoting social justice during his caliphate significantly impacted the development of Islam.

Challenges and Controversies: His later reign faced internal political complexities and criticisms, offering valuable lessons in leadership during turbulent times.

Religious and Personal Life: Examining his piety, relationship with Prophet Muhammad (ﷺ)(PBUH), and personal conduct provides a holistic understanding of his character and motivations.

Further Exploration and Continuous Learning:

Uthman Ibn Affan's life invites further exploration on various levels:

In-depth studies of specific business ventures: Examining specific trade routes, partnerships, and innovative strategies employed by Uthman can offer practical insights for contemporary entrepreneurs.

Comparative analysis with other prominent Muslim merchants: Exploring the approaches of contemporaries like Khadija bint Khuwaylid and Abd al-Rahman ibn Awf can provide richer context and comparative perspectives.

Application of his principles to contemporary challenges: Engaging in dialogue on how Uthman's ethical principles and social responsibility can be applied to address modern-day economic and social concerns can foster meaningful learning and positive change.

By delving deeper into the multifaceted life of Uthman Ibn Affan, we gain valuable insights not just into the history of Islamic trade but also into timeless principles of ethical leadership, responsible business practices

Upon learning of the Prophet's declaration regarding the well in Paradise being reserved for whoever secures it for the community, 'Uthman ibn 'Affan took action. He approached the owner and offered to purchase the well, but the owner declined. 'Uthman then proposed buying half of it or renting it, with alternate days designated for Muslims and the owner's personal use. The owner agreed to this arrangement.

As a result, everyone flocked to drink from the well on 'Uthman's designated day, leaving the owner without customers. Feeling the impact, the owner hastened to 'Uthman and pleaded, "You have disrupted my business; please buy the well from me." 'Uthman agreed, purchasing it for 20 thousand dirhams, which he then dedicated as an endowment (waqf) in the name of Allah for the benefit of all Muslims.

Hazrat Usman (RA), famously known as 'Ghani' for his immense wealth and generosity, was a prominent figure in Islamic history. He earned the title 'Zunnoorain,' meaning 'possessing two lights,' for his marriage to two of the Prophet Muhammad (SAW)'s daughters, Ruqayyah (RA) and Umm Kulthum (RA). Additionally, Hazrat Usman

(RA) was blessed with seven children. He holds the esteemed status of being one of the 'Ashrah Mubashsharah'—the ten companions guaranteed Paradise by the Prophet Muhammad (SAW).

Total wealth of Uthman Ibn Affan

According to Mas'udi in his Muruju'dh-Dhahab, Volume I, page 433, and other historians, Uthman was known for constructing an elaborate stone house adorned with sandalwood doors. He accumulated significant wealth, which he generously bestowed upon the Umayyads and others. For instance, he allocated the religious levy (Khums) from Armenia, a region conquered during his reign, to Marwan without religious authorization. Additionally, he granted Marwan 100,000 dirhams from the Baitu'l-Mal (the public treasury). Abdallah bin Khalid received 400,000 dirhams, Hakam bin Abi'l-As—cursed and banished by the Prophet—received 100,000 dirhams, and Abu Sufyan received 200,000 dirhams, as documented by Ibn Abi'l-Hadid in his Sharhe Nahju'l-Balagha, Volume I, page 68.

On the day of his assassination, Uthman's personal wealth totaled 150,000 dinars and 20 million dirhams in cash. He also owned property in Wadiu'l-Qura and Hunain valued at 100,000 dinars, along with extensive herds of cattle, sheep, and camels. However, his actions led to the accumulation of vast wealth by the prominent Umayyads at the expense of the general populace.

Total Dirham - 800000+44400000 (20million) = 45200000 (1 Dirham is 3.0gram) 45200000*3=135600000 Gram, in USD 1633586.76
Total Dinar = 100000+150000=250000*4.25=1062500 gram
1 gram 65.02508 $ - 1062500*65.02508= 69089124.125 USD
Total - USD 1633586.76+69089124.125 = 70722710.885

The dinar was 4.25 grams of 22k gold, while the dirham was 3.0 grams of pure silver. Umar Ibn al-Khattab established the standard relationship between the two coins, stating that "7 dinars must be equivalent to 10 dirhams".

1 gram silver coin price in USD 0.74 $
3gram Silver coin (Dirham) USD 0.74*3 = $ 2.22

Uthman ibn Affan assumed the position of the third Caliph after the demise of Umar ibn Al-Khattab. Throughout his caliphate, he accomplished several significant feats:

Expansion of the Islamic State:
Under Uthman's leadership, the Islamic realm witnessed numerous conquests aimed at extending the influence of Islam across various regions. These conquests included Murrow, Turkey, Alexandria, Armenia, Caucasus, Khurasan, Kerman, Africa, and Cyprus, contributing to the global dissemination of Islam.

Expansion of Al-Masjid Al-Nabawi:

Uthman undertook the expansion of Al-Masjid Al-Nabawi, the Prophet's Mosque, enhancing its capacity to accommodate worshippers and facilitate community gatherings.

Establishment of the First Islamic Fleet:
Recognizing the threat posed by Byzantine attacks on Islamic shores, Uthman established the inaugural Islamic fleet. This fleet played a crucial role in safeguarding the Islamic territories from external threats and maintaining maritime security.

Compilation of the Quran:
Among Uthman's most notable achievements was the completion of the Compilation of the Quran. Although initiated during the caliphate of Abu Bakr Siddiq, it was under Uthman's guidance that the compilation was finalized. This monumental effort ensured the preservation and standardization of the Quranic text, safeguarding it from potential discrepancies or alterations.

Uthman ibn Affan's contributions to the expansion of the Islamic state, the enhancement of religious infrastructure, the establishment of maritime defense, and the preservation of the Quran solidified his legacy as a visionary leader and a key figure in the history of Islam.

Due to the expansion of the Islamic reign many of the new Muslims were not Arabic speakers. Therefore in order to help them all recite the holy Quran correctly Uthman made copies of the holy Quran and distributed it.

Hudhaifah (R.A.) said to Uthman (R.A.):

"O Prince of Believers, save this nation before they differ concerning the Book (Quran) as the Jews and the Christians did."

Uthman (R.A.) said:

"Send us the manuscript so that we may make copies of it, then we will return it to you".

Once upon a time, during a crucial battle, the beloved Prophet Muhammad (peace be upon him) turned to Usman ibn Affan and asked, "How much do you wish to contribute?" Usman, known for his boundless generosity, humbly replied, "Whatever you advise, O Messenger of Allah." With a knowing smile, the Prophet suggested a hundred camels.

However, the Prophet's words held a deeper meaning, one that Usman understood well. Recognizing the opportunity for immense spiritual reward, Usman returned with a staggering contribution: a thousand loaded camels, seventy horses, and ten thousand dinars. Such was Usman's unwavering dedication to the cause of Islam, as chronicled by Imam Kastalani in Al-Muwahib al-Ladunniyyah.

During Hazrat Umar's caliphate, when three years of scarcity struck, Usman once again demonstrated his generosity. He contributed grain, loaded on camels, stretching from Saudi Arabia to Egypt. One can only imagine the remarkable sight of this caravan of camels, stretching across vast distances to deliver aid to those in need.

Usman's remarkable contributions to Islam exemplify the power of business in serving humanity. Despite his vast wealth, he remained humble and dedicated, always ready to lend a helping hand to those in need. His actions serve as a timeless reminder of the profound impact that generosity and compassion can have on the world.

The Dazzling Trade Empire of Khadija bint Khuwaylid: a Pioneering Businesswoman

Khadija bint Khuwaylid, often hailed as the first Muslim woman and the wife of Prophet Muhammad (ﷺ)(PBUH), wasn't merely a historical figure; she was a revolutionary businesswoman who shattered societal norms and established a trading empire that captivated Mecca. This essay delves into her remarkable business acumen, exploring how she rose through the ranks, shaped Islamic commerce, and continues to inspire generations of entrepreneurs.

A Legacy Carved in Trade:

Born into a powerful Meccan tribe known for trade, Khadija inherited a keen business sense from her father. Unlike most women of her time confined to domestic roles, she actively pursued a career, becoming a renowned merchant known for her intelligence, integrity, and fairness.

By the time she met Prophet Muhammad (ﷺ)(PBUH), she had already established a diverse and flourishing trade network, earning the epithet "Khadija the Great" and the respect of the entire Quraysh tribe.

Keys to her Success: Pillars of Ethical Trade:

Khadija's business acumen wasn't just about amassing wealth; it was built on solid ethical principles that became hallmarks of Islamic commerce:

Fairness and Integrity: She earned the trust of clients through scrupulous honesty and fair pricing. Deception and exploitation had no place in her transactions, building a reputation for reliability and ethical conduct.

Discerning Judgment and Strategic Partnerships: Recognizing potential, she partnered with trustworthy individuals, expanding her reach and expertise. Her partnerships weren't solely driven by profit; she valued personal integrity and shared values in her associates.

Innovation and Diversification: Not limited to traditional trade routes, Khadija ventured into new territories, diversifying her portfolio with goods like silk, spices, and slaves. This adaptability and risk management ensured her empire's continued growth and resilience.

Social Responsibility and Philanthropy: Wealth wasn't just for personal gain; Khadija actively supported the less fortunate, funding public works, providing dowries for women, and assisting widows and orphans. This generosity stemmed from her faith and deep-rooted belief in social responsibility.

A Catalyst for Change: Empowering Women and Shaping Trade Practices:

Khadija's success defied societal norms, paving the way for other women to participate in trade. She challenged the perception of women as solely confined to domestic spheres, demonstrating their capability and potential in the economic realm. This empowered other women to pursue their ambitions and contributed to a shift in social attitudes towards female entrepreneurship.

Beyond individual empowerment, Khadija's influence extended to shaping the very fabric of Islamic commerce. Her commitment to ethical practices, fair trade, and social responsibility laid the foundation for principles that continue to guide Muslim merchants today.

Beyond Merchantship: A Supportive Partner and Pillar of Faith:

While her business acumen was exceptional, Khadija's legacy transcends her commercial success. She recognized the potential of Prophet Muhammad (ﷺ)(PBUH), becoming his first follower and offering unwavering support throughout his mission. Her financial security shielded him from persecution and enabled him to dedicate himself to spreading Islam. This unwavering support proved crucial in the early days of Islam, solidifying her role as a significant figure in religious history.

Lessons for Modern Entrepreneurs: A Timeless Legacy:

The life and achievements of Khadija offer valuable lessons for aspiring entrepreneurs and leaders, regardless of their faith or gender:

Integrity and ethical conduct are foundations for sustainable success. Building trust and loyalty through fair dealing and honesty remains paramount in today's competitive environment.

Discernment and strategic partnerships are key to expanding reach and expertise. Recognizing potential in others and collaborating with individuals who share your values strengthens your venture.

Innovation and adaptability are crucial for navigating a dynamic market. Embracing change and exploring new opportunities can create a competitive edge.

Social responsibility fosters positive change and strengthens your community. Integrating ethical practices and giving back to society can solidify your positive impact.

Looking Beyond the Surface: Exploring Specifics and Deeper Connections:

A nuanced understanding of Khadija's life necessitates delving deeper:

Examining specific challenges she faced: Analyzing how she navigated challenges in a male-dominated society and overcame hurdles in pursuing her ambitions can offer valuable insights for women entrepreneurs today.

Exploring the complexities of her partnerships: Studying specific partnerships, with figures like Maysarah, can provide practical lessons on collaboration, risk management, and building trust in business relationships.

Connecting her business practices to broader historical context: Understanding the economic and social landscape of Mecca during her time helps appreciate the significance of her achievements and their impact on the region.

Continuing Legacy and Ongoing Inspiration:

Khadija bint Khuwaylid wasn't just a successful businesswoman; she was a visionary leader, a pioneer for women's empowerment, and a pillar of strength for Prophet Muhammad (ﷺ)(P

Abu Talib: The Shadow Behind the Prophet - Exploring His Business Life

Abu Talib ibn Abd al-Muttalib (c. 535 – 619 CE) stands as a complex figure in early Islamic history. While not a convert to Islam himself, he played a pivotal role in the life of Prophet Muhammad (ﷺ)(PBUH), serving as his uncle, guardian, and constant protector during the challenging early years of the faith. While often overshadowed by the Prophet's journey, Abu Talib's own life, particularly his successful career as a merchant, offers valuable insights into the socio-economic landscape of

Mecca and the challenges faced by traders in pre-Islamic Arabia.

A Lineage Steeped in Commerce:

Born into the esteemed Hashim clan of the Quraysh tribe, renowned for their trade networks, Abu Talib inherited a strong commercial background. He honed his skills through involvement in various ventures, primarily operating within the Arabian Peninsula. He led caravans along established trade routes like the frankincense trade route, transporting valuable commodities like spices, silk, and other luxury goods.

Beyond Trade: Leadership and Civic Duties:

Abu Talib wasn't just a successful merchant; he held prestigious positions within Meccan society. He served as the leader of the Hashim clan, inheriting the position after his father's death. This role entrusted him with responsibility for the clan's welfare, representing them in disputes, negotiating alliances, and managing communal resources. Additionally, he served as the custodian of the Kaaba, the central religious site in Mecca, demonstrating his position of trust and respect within the community.

Navigating a Complex Economy:

The Meccan economy of Abu Talib's time was dynamic but fraught with challenges. Trade routes were vulnerable to banditry, political instability could disrupt markets, and competition was fierce. To navigate these complexities, Abu Talib likely employed astute skills:

Developing Strong Partnerships: He likely collaborated with reliable merchants, forming partnerships to share resources, information, and protection on caravans.
Diversifying Investments: He wouldn't have put all his eggs in one basket, likely investing in various commodities and trade routes to minimize risk.
Building Trust and Reputation: Honesty, fair dealing, and fulfilling agreements were crucial for building trust with clients and fellow merchants in a community where reputation was key.
Challenges and Ethical Considerations:

While achieving success, Abu Talib also faced ethical dilemmas typical of pre-Islamic Arabia. Interest rates on loans could be exorbitant, and some trade practices might exploit less powerful merchants. However, some accounts suggest Abu Talib prioritized fairness and avoided usury, earning him respect even from non-Muslims.

Beyond Personal Success: Impact on the Prophet:

While Abu Talib never embraced Islam himself, his role in Prophet Muhammad's life was vital. He provided financial support during Muhammad's early years as a merchant, offered protection during persecution, and remained a steadfast source of emotional support. This unwavering support during the most challenging phase of Islam's emergence had a lasting impact on the faith's development.

Shifting Tides: Challenges and Controversies:

Abu Talib's unwavering support for his nephew despite not converting himself strained his relationship with other Quraysh leaders, who opposed Islam's growing influence. As tensions escalated, he faced increasing pressure to denounce his nephew's message, leading to accusations of hypocrisy and opportunism from some historians.

Legacy and Unanswered Questions:

Abu Talib's life, particularly his business success, offers valuable insights into the pre-Islamic Arabian economy and the challenges faced by merchants. However, several questions remain:

The extent of his ethical practices compared to his contemporaries is subject to debate, requiring further historical analysis.
His motivations for not converting to Islam despite his close relationship with the Prophet continue to be an area of scholarly exploration.
The impact of his economic success on the early Muslim community necessitates further study.
Beyond Business: A Holistic Understanding:

Understanding Abu Talib solely through his business life offers a limited perspective. Exploring his role as a leader, family man, and confidante to the Prophet provides a more complete picture of his complex and multifaceted legacy.

Delving deeper into Abu Talib's life can foster valuable learning:

Studying specific trade routes and practices employed by Abu Talib can offer insights into pre-Islamic Arabian commerce.
Examining his leadership approach within the Quraysh and his diplomatic negotiations provide lessons in navigating complex social and political realities.
Analyzing his relationship with the Prophet sheds light on the dynamics of family, faith, and personal convictions in challenging times.
Abu Talib's life, though veiled in some aspects, remains a window into a crucial period of Islamic history. By moving beyond simplistic interpretations and engaging in nuanced explorations, we gain valuable insights not just into business practices of the past

Abd al-Rahman ibn Awf: Successful Trader and Treasurer of the Muslim Community

Introduction:

Abd al-Rahman ibn Awf, one of the prominent companions of the Prophet Muhammad (ﷺ)(peace be upon him), played a significant role in the early Muslim community as both a successful trader and a trusted treasurer. His life and achievements exemplify the values of integrity, entrepreneurship, and generosity that characterize the best of Islamic commerce. This essay explores the remarkable journey of Abd al-Rahman ibn Awf, his contributions to trade and finance, and the enduring legacy he left for generations to come.

Early Life and Conversion:

Abd al-Rahman ibn Awf was born into the Banu Zuhrah tribe of the Quraysh in Mecca, a prominent clan known for its commercial prowess. Little is known about his early life, but it is believed that he grew up in a mercantile environment, learning the intricacies of trade from a young age. In his youth, Abd al-Rahman was known for his intelligence, shrewdness, and keen business acumen.

Abd al-Rahman's life took a transformative turn with the advent of Islam. Like many of his contemporaries, he was initially skeptical of the new faith preached by Muhammad, but he eventually embraced Islam after witnessing the sincerity and conviction of the Prophet. His conversion marked the beginning of a new chapter in his life, one characterized by unwavering faith and unwavering commitment to the principles of Islam.

Success in Trade:

Abd al-Rahman ibn Awf quickly established himself as a successful trader in the bustling markets of Mecca. He possessed a natural talent for commerce, coupled with a strong work ethic and a keen understanding of market dynamics. His ventures in trade brought him considerable wealth and prestige, earning him a reputation as one of the most prosperous merchants in the city.

One of Abd al-Rahman's most notable business ventures was his involvement in the caravan trade, a lucrative enterprise that involved transporting goods between Mecca and distant markets in Syria and beyond. He participated in numerous trading expeditions, navigating the treacherous desert routes with skill and determination. His success in trade brought him into contact with merchants from diverse backgrounds, enriching his knowledge and expanding his network of contacts.

Migration to Medina:

With the growing persecution of Muslims in Mecca, Abd al-Rahman ibn Awf, like many other believers, decided to migrate to Medina in search of safety and freedom to practice their faith. His migration marked a turning point in his life, as he became intimately involved in the affairs of the nascent Muslim community led by the Prophet Muhammad.

In Medina, Abd al-Rahman's skills as a trader and financier proved invaluable to the Muslim community, which was in need of resources to support its growing population and burgeoning infrastructure. He used his wealth and expertise to contribute to the welfare of the community, providing financial assistance to the needy, funding military expeditions, and investing in various development projects.

Trustworthiness and Integrity:

One of the defining qualities of Abd al-Rahman ibn Awf was his unwavering trustworthiness and integrity in financial matters. He was known for his honesty, reliability, and adherence to ethical principles in all his dealings. His reputation for integrity earned him the trust and respect of his fellow Muslims, as well as the confidence of the Prophet Muhammad (ﷺ)himself.

Abd al-Rahman's integrity was put to the test on numerous occasions, particularly during his tenure as the treasurer of the Muslim community. As the custodian of the community's wealth, he handled large sums of money with the utmost care and diligence, ensuring transparency and accountability in financial transactions. His scrupulousness in financial matters set a high standard for ethical conduct in Islamic finance.

Contributions to the Muslim Community:

Abd al-Rahman ibn Awf made significant contributions to the welfare and development of the Muslim community during his lifetime. As a successful trader and financier, he provided financial support to the Prophet Muhammad (ﷺ)and his companions, enabling them to fulfill their mission of spreading Islam and establishing a just society based on the principles of faith and righteousness.

One of Abd al-Rahman's most notable contributions was his participation in the Bayt al-Mal, or the treasury of the Muslim community, which was responsible for managing the financial affairs of the state. He served as a treasurer of the Bayt al-Mal under the caliphs Abu Bakr and Umar, overseeing the collection, distribution, and allocation of funds for various purposes, including welfare, infrastructure development, and defense.

Generosity and Philanthropy:

Abd al-Rahman ibn Awf was renowned for his generosity and philanthropy, particularly towards the less fortunate members of society. He was known to be a charitable donor, contributing generously to charitable causes and supporting those in need with food, clothing, and financial assistance. His acts of kindness and compassion endeared him to the hearts of the people, earning him a reputation as a benefactor and patron of the needy.

One of the most famous anecdotes illustrating Abd al-Rahman's generosity is the story of his donation to the Muslim army during the Battle of Tabuk. When the Prophet Muhammad (ﷺ) called upon his companions to contribute to the military expedition, Abd al-Rahman came forward with a substantial donation of 4,000 dinars, demonstrating his unwavering commitment to the cause of

Islam and his willingness to sacrifice his wealth for the greater good.

Enduring Legacy:

The legacy of Abd al-Rahman ibn Awf as a successful trader and treasurer of the Muslim community continues to inspire generations of Muslims to this day. His exemplary conduct, entrepreneurial spirit, and philanthropic generosity serve as a model for ethical commerce and responsible stewardship of wealth in Islam. His life story underscores the importance of integrity, trustworthiness, and social responsibility in business and finance, values that remain relevant and timeless in today's world.

In conclusion, Abd al-Rahman ibn Awf stands as a shining example of a successful trader and treasurer who combined worldly success with spiritual fulfillment. His life journey from a humble merchant in Mecca to a trusted advisor and benefactor of the Muslim community in Medina exemplifies the transformative power of faith and the profound impact that individuals can have on the course of history. As Muslims strive to uphold the values of integrity, honesty, and compassion in their commercial endeavors, they can draw inspiration from the life and legacy of Abd al-Rahman ibn Awf, whose name will forever be remembered as a beacon of light and guidance in the annals of Islamic history.

Sa'd ibn Abi Waqqas: Trader, Courageous Warrior, and Inspirational Leader

Sa'd ibn Abi Waqqas, a prominent figure in early Islamic history, is renowned for his multifaceted contributions as a trader, courageous warrior, and inspirational leader. Born into the illustrious Banu Zuhrah clan of the Quraysh tribe in Mecca, Sa'd emerged as a key companion of the Prophet Muhammad (ﷺ)(peace be upon him) and played pivotal roles in various aspects of Islamic life. This comprehensive essay delves into the life, achievements, and legacy of Sa'd ibn Abi Waqqas, examining his prowess as a trader, his valor on the battlefield, and his exemplary leadership qualities.

Early Life and Background:

Sa'd ibn Abi Waqqas was born in Mecca around 595 CE to the Banu Zuhrah clan of the Quraysh tribe, a lineage renowned for its nobility and distinction. His father, Abu Waqqas ibn Abd Manaf, was a respected member of the Quraysh aristocracy, while his mother, Hamnah bint Sufyan, hailed from a distinguished lineage. From a young age, Sa'd demonstrated intelligence, courage, and determination, traits that would shape his future endeavors as a trader, warrior, and leader within the Islamic community.

Early Encounters with Islam:

Saʿd's first encounter with Islam occurred during the early days of the prophetic mission of Muhammad (ﷺ)(peace be upon him). Influenced by the teachings of his maternal uncle, Al-Aswad ibn Abd Yaghuth, Saʿd embraced Islam at a relatively young age, becoming one of the earliest converts to the faith. His unwavering commitment to Islam earned him the admiration and respect of the Prophet Muhammad (ﷺ)and positioned him as a trusted companion and advisor.

Role as a Trader:

Prior to his embrace of Islam, Saʿd was involved in trade and commerce, a profession deeply ingrained in the economic fabric of Meccan society. His business acumen, shrewdness, and integrity made him a successful trader, and he accumulated wealth and influence through his commercial ventures. Even after embracing Islam, Saʿd continued to engage in trade, albeit with a renewed sense of ethical responsibility and adherence to Islamic principles of fairness and justice.

Contributions to Islamic Trade:

As a devout Muslim and seasoned trader, Sa'd played a crucial role in expanding Islamic trade networks and fostering economic growth within the Muslim community. He participated in numerous trade caravans, establishing commercial connections with neighboring regions and contributing to the prosperity of the fledgling Muslim ummah. Sa'd's ethical conduct, honesty, and integrity set a high standard for business dealings among early Muslims, earning him the title of "Sa'd the Honest."

Courageous Warrior:

Sa'd ibn Abi Waqqas distinguished himself as a courageous and skilled warrior on the battlefield, earning him a place among the most esteemed companions of the Prophet Muhammad. He participated in several major battles, including the Battle of Badr, the Battle of Uhud, and the Battle of the Trench, demonstrating valor, steadfastness, and unwavering commitment to the cause of Islam. Sa'd's leadership and bravery inspired his fellow Muslims and contributed to the success of pivotal military campaigns.

Leadership Qualities:

Throughout his life, Sa'd exemplified exemplary leadership qualities that endeared him to his peers and earned him the respect and admiration of the Prophet Muhammad. His humility, wisdom, and ability to lead by example set him apart as a role model for future generations of Muslims. Sa'd's leadership extended beyond the battlefield to various aspects of community life, where he served as a trusted advisor, arbitrator, and mentor to his fellow companions.

Contributions to Islamic Scholarship:

In addition to his military and commercial pursuits, Sa'd ibn Abi Waqqas made significant contributions to Islamic scholarship and jurisprudence. He was renowned for his knowledge of the Quran, Hadith, and Islamic law, and he played a key role in transmitting and preserving the teachings of Islam for future generations. Sa'd's expertise and insights were sought after by his contemporaries and continue to be revered by scholars of Islam to this day.

Later Years and Legacy:

In his later years, Sa'd ibn Abi Waqqas continued to serve the Muslim community in various capacities, offering counsel, guidance, and support to his fellow companions and successors. He played a prominent role in the selection of the caliphs Abu Bakr and Umar ibn al-Khattab and remained an influential figure within the early Islamic state.

Sa'd's legacy endured long after his passing, as his exemplary life and achievements continued to inspire Muslims across generations.

Sa'd ibn Abi Waqqas, revered as a trader, courageous warrior, and inspirational leader, occupies a cherished place in Islamic history and tradition. His unwavering commitment to Islam, ethical conduct in commerce, valor on the battlefield, exemplary leadership qualities, and contributions to Islamic scholarship exemplify the highest ideals of faith, integrity, and service. Sa'd's life and legacy serve as a timeless testament to the enduring values and principles of Islam, inspiring Muslims around the world to emulate his example and strive for excellence in all aspects of life.

Talha ibn Abdullah: A Wealthy Merchant and Valiant Warrior

In the tapestry of early Islamic history, Talha ibn Abdullah (598-656 CE) stands out as a figure of multifaceted accomplishments. A successful merchant renowned for his generosity, he actively participated in pivotal battles, demonstrating unwavering courage and leadership. However, his legacy remains complex, intertwined with political controversies and internal conflicts within the Muslim community. Exploring his life offers valuable insights into the intersection of commerce, faith, and the complexities of navigating historical events.

Early Life and Business Acumen:

Born into a prominent Meccan family, Talha possessed a keen mind for trade from a young age. He established extensive trade networks across the Arabian Peninsula, amassing significant wealth through astute business practices. renowned for their expertise in the lucrative silk trade, Talha inherited a strong foundation for his own commercial endeavors. He honed his skills in international trade, venturing beyond the Arabian Peninsula to establish trade networks spanning Syria, Yemen, and even parts of Africa. These ventures yielded him immense wealth, solidifying his reputation as a successful merchant.

Known for his fairness and generosity, he earned the respect of both Muslims and non-Muslims, solidifying his reputation as a prominent figure in Meccan society.

Embracing Islam and Supporting the Prophet:

Despite his comfortable life, Talha embraced Islam readily, becoming one of the early companions of Prophet Muhammad (ﷺ)(PBUH). He actively supported the fledgling Muslim community, offering financial assistance during their challenging years in Mecca. His unwavering faith and loyalty led him to participate in the migration to Madinah (Hijrah), sacrificing his established life for the sake of his beliefs.

A Warrior on the Battlefield:

Talha's courage and leadership shone brightly on the battlefield. He participated in numerous significant battles alongside the Prophet, including the pivotal Battle of Badr and the conquest of Khaybar. His bravery earned him the admiration of his fellow warriors, solidifying his reputation as a formidable defender of the faith.

Beyond Military Prowess: Stepping into Leadership:

Following the Prophet's passing, Talha actively participated in the political landscape of the nascent Muslim community. He held prominent positions during the caliphates of Abu Bakr and Umar, contributing to the consolidation and expansion of the Islamic empire. His administrative skills and political acumen earned him the trust of the caliphs and respect within the community.

Controversies and Complexities:

However, Talha's legacy is not without its controversies. He played a key role in the Battle of the Camel, a major internal conflict within the Muslim community. While his motivations remain debated, his involvement in this conflict tarnished his image for some and continues to be a subject of historical and religious analysis.

A Life Intertwined with Trade and Faith:

Throughout his life, Talha skillfully navigated the intersection of commerce and faith:

Using Wealth for the Community: His financial resources benefited the Muslim community immensely. He supported those in need, contributed to public works, and funded expeditions, demonstrating his commitment to social responsibility.

Ethical Practices in Trade: Despite his significant wealth, Talha was known for his fair and honest dealings in the marketplace. He upheld Islamic principles in his business transactions, maintaining integrity even amidst competition.

Balancing Faith and Worldly Pursuits: While actively involved in trade and politics, Talha remained devoted to his faith. He participated in religious practices, contributed to the preservation of Islamic knowledge, and strived to live a life guided by his beliefs.

Lessons for Modern Times: Beyond Historical Narrative:

Talha ibn Abdullah's life offers valuable lessons for individuals navigating various domains:

Entrepreneurship with Social Responsibility: His commitment to ethical trade and utilizing wealth for the betterment of the community serves as a model for modern entrepreneurs seeking to integrate social responsibility into their business practices.

Courage and Leadership, but Understanding Nuances: Talha's bravery and leadership inspire, but engaging with the complexities of his involvement in the Battle of the Camel encourages critical thinking and nuanced understanding of historical events.

Faith as a Guiding Force: His life exemplifies the power of faith in shaping actions and contributions to society, encouraging individuals to live their values with purpose and integrity.

Further Exploration: Deepening Our Understanding:

Engaging with Talha's life in greater depth can enrich our understanding:

Examining Specific Battles and Political Events: Studying his role in key battles and political decisions, including the Battle of the Camel, can offer valuable insights into leadership under pressure and the complexities of navigating internal conflicts.

Exploring Diverse Interpretations: Analyzing how historians and religious scholars interpret Talha's actions and motivations can provide a richer understanding of his legacy and the multiplicity of perspectives surrounding him.

Applying Lessons to Contemporary Challenges: Reflecting on how Talha's principles of ethical business, responsible leadership, and navigating complex situations can be applied to address contemporary social, political, and economic challenges can foster meaningful learning and positive change.

Talha ibn Abdullah's life transcends a mere historical account. He serves as a reminder that the human experience is multifaceted, often encompassing remarkable achievements alongside controversial aspects. By delving deeper into his legacy, we gain valuable insights into the

Khuzaymah ibn Thabit: Skilled Scribe, Astute Merchant, and Faithful Companion of the Prophet Muhammad

Khuzaymah ibn Thabit, a revered figure in early Islamic history, is celebrated for his multifaceted contributions as a skilled scribe, astute merchant, and faithful companion of the Prophet Muhammad (ﷺ)(peace be upon him). Born into the illustrious Thabit clan of the Aws tribe in Medina, Khuzaymah emerged as a key supporter of Islam and played pivotal roles in various aspects of the Islamic community. This comprehensive essay explores the life, achievements, and legacy of Khuzaymah ibn Thabit, highlighting his proficiency as a scribe, his acumen as a merchant, and his unwavering devotion to Islam.

Early Life and Background:

Khuzaymah ibn Thabit was born into the Thabit clan of the Aws tribe in Medina, a city that would later become the epicenter of Islam. Little is known about his early life, but it is believed that he grew up in a household known for its piety, learning, and noble lineage. From a young age, Khuzaymah displayed a keen intellect, a strong sense of moral integrity, and a deep reverence for the teachings of Islam, traits that would define his later contributions to the Muslim community.

Role as a Skilled Scribe:

Khuzaymah ibn Thabit distinguished himself as a skilled scribe, possessing exceptional proficiency in reading, writing, and documenting important matters. In the early days of Islam, when literacy was relatively rare, Khuzaymah's abilities as a scribe were highly valued and sought after by his fellow companions and leaders of the Muslim community. He played a crucial role in recording and preserving the revelations of the Quran, transcribing the words of the Prophet Muhammad (ﷺ) with accuracy and precision.

Contributions to Islamic Scholarship:

As a skilled scribe, Khuzaymah ibn Thabit made invaluable contributions to Islamic scholarship and knowledge dissemination. He played a pivotal role in the compilation and preservation of the Quran, ensuring that the divine revelations were accurately recorded and transmitted to future generations. Khuzaymah's meticulous attention to detail, reverence for the sacred texts, and commitment to scholarly integrity earned him the respect and admiration of his contemporaries and successors.

Role as a Merchant:

In addition to his scholarly pursuits, Khuzaymah ibn Thabit was also known for his acumen as a merchant, engaging in trade and commerce to support himself and his family. His business ventures took him across the Arabian Peninsula, where he established commercial connections and traded in goods ranging from textiles to spices. Despite his success as a merchant, Khuzaymah remained humble and grounded, never allowing worldly pursuits to distract him from his spiritual obligations.

Encounter with Islam:

Khuzaymah ibn Thabit's encounter with Islam occurred during the early years of the prophetic mission of Muhammad (ﷺ)(peace be upon him). Influenced by the message of monotheism, justice, and compassion preached by the Prophet, Khuzaymah embraced Islam with sincerity and conviction, becoming one of the earliest converts to the faith. His unwavering commitment to Islam and his close association with the Prophet Muhammad (ﷺ)earned him the esteemed title of "Khuzaymah the Faithful."

Participation in Community Affairs:

Khuzaymah ibn Thabit actively participated in various community affairs, serving as a trusted advisor, mediator, and arbitrator among his fellow companions. He played a key role in resolving disputes, reconciling differences, and upholding the principles of justice and equity within the Muslim community. Khuzaymah's impartiality, wisdom, and integrity made him a beloved and respected figure among his peers and contributed to the cohesion and stability of early Islamic society.

Legacy and Influence:

Khuzaymah ibn Thabit's legacy endures as a testament to the enduring values and principles of Islam, inspiring Muslims around the world to emulate his example of piety, scholarship, and service to humanity. His contributions as a skilled scribe, astute merchant, and faithful companion of the Prophet Muhammad (ﷺ)exemplify the highest ideals of faith, integrity, and devotion to God. Khuzaymah's life and legacy continue to serve as a source of inspiration and guidance for Muslims seeking to uphold the teachings of Islam in their daily lives.

Khuzaymah ibn Thabit, celebrated as a skilled scribe, astute merchant, and faithful companion of the Prophet Muhammad, occupies a revered place in Islamic history and tradition. His proficiency as a scribe, acumen as a merchant, and unwavering devotion to Islam exemplify the highest ideals of faith, integrity, and service to humanity. Khuzaymah's contributions to Islamic scholarship, community affairs, and the preservation of the Quran serve as a timeless testament to the enduring values and principles of Islam, inspiring Muslims around the world to emulate his example and strive for excellence in all aspects of life.

Abdur-Rahman ibn Harith: Merchant, Early Convert to Islam, and Participant in the Migration to Medina

Abdur-Rahman ibn Harith, a prominent figure in early Islamic history, is revered for his multifaceted contributions as a merchant, early convert to Islam, and participant in the migration to Medina. Born into a noble and affluent family in Mecca, Abdur-Rahman emerged as a key supporter of Islam and played pivotal roles in various aspects of the Islamic community. This comprehensive essay explores the life, achievements, and legacy of Abdur-Rahman ibn Harith, highlighting his prowess as a merchant, his commitment to Islam, and his role in the migration to Medina.

Early Life and Background:

Abdur-Rahman ibn Harith was born into a prominent and affluent family in Mecca, a city renowned for its commercial and religious significance. Little is known about his early life, but it is believed that he grew up in a household known for its wealth, influence, and adherence to traditional Arab customs and values. From a young age, Abdur-Rahman displayed intelligence, resilience, and a keen interest in commerce, traits that would shape his future endeavors as a merchant and supporter of Islam.

Role as a Merchant:

Abdur-Rahman ibn Harith distinguished himself as a successful and enterprising merchant, engaging in trade and commerce to support himself and his family. His business ventures took him across the Arabian Peninsula, where he established commercial connections and traded in goods ranging from textiles to spices. Despite his success as a merchant, Abdur-Rahman remained humble and grounded, never allowing worldly pursuits to distract him from his spiritual obligations.

Encounter with Islam:

Abdur-Rahman ibn Harith's encounter with Islam occurred during the early years of the prophetic mission of Muhammad (ﷺ)(peace be upon him). Influenced by the message of monotheism, social justice, and moral righteousness preached by the Prophet, Abdur-Rahman embraced Islam with sincerity and conviction, becoming one of the earliest converts to the faith. His unwavering commitment to Islam and his close association with the Prophet Muhammad (ﷺ)earned him the esteemed title of "Abdur-Rahman the Faithful."

Participation in the Migration to Medina:

Abdur-Rahman ibn Harith played a crucial role in the migration (hijrah) from Mecca to Medina, a watershed event in Islamic history that marked the establishment of the first Islamic state. Along with the Prophet Muhammad (ﷺ)and other early Muslims, Abdur-Rahman bravely journeyed to Medina in search of religious freedom, social justice, and community solidarity. His participation in the migration demonstrated his unwavering commitment to Islam and his willingness to sacrifice personal comfort for the sake of his faith.

Contributions to the Muslim Community:

In addition to his role as a merchant and early convert to Islam, Abdur-Rahman ibn Harith made significant contributions to the Muslim community, serving as a trusted advisor, mediator, and arbitrator among his fellow companions. He played a key role in resolving disputes, reconciling differences, and upholding the principles of justice and equity within the Muslim community. Abdur-Rahman's impartiality, wisdom, and integrity made him a beloved and respected figure among his peers and contributed to the cohesion and stability of early Islamic society.

Legacy and Influence:

Abdur-Rahman ibn Harith's legacy endures as a testament to the enduring values and principles of Islam, inspiring Muslims around the world to emulate his example of piety, resilience, and commitment to social justice. His contributions as a merchant, early convert to Islam, and participant in the migration to Medina exemplify the highest ideals of faith, integrity, and devotion to God. Abdur-Rahman's life and legacy continue to serve as a source of inspiration and guidance for Muslims seeking to uphold the teachings of Islam in their daily lives.

Abdur-Rahman ibn Harith, celebrated as a merchant, early convert to Islam, and participant in the migration to Medina, occupies a revered place in Islamic history and tradition. His prowess as a merchant, commitment to Islam, and role in the migration to Medina exemplify the highest ideals of faith, resilience, and devotion to God. Abdur-Rahman's contributions to the Muslim community and his unwavering dedication to the principles of justice and equity serve as a timeless testament to the enduring values of Islam, inspiring Muslims around the world to emulate his example and strive for excellence in all aspects of life.

Abdur Rahman ibn Awf's Remarkable Generosity

Abdurrahman ibn Awf, a revered companion of the Prophet Muhammad (peace be upon him), exemplified unparalleled generosity and selflessness, particularly in the service of Allah and the Muslim community. His benevolence and magnanimity were renowned during the Prophet's lifetime, leaving an indelible mark on Islamic history.

Substantial Charitable Contributions:
Abdurrahman ibn Awf's generosity knew no bounds, as he willingly sacrificed a significant portion of his wealth for the sake of Allah. On three separate occasions, he gave away half of his property, demonstrating his unwavering commitment to charity and philanthropy. Notably, he distributed 4000 dirhams, 40,000 dirhams, and 40,000 gold coins on these occasions, showcasing his extraordinary generosity and devotion to the cause of Islam.

Liberation of Captives and Military Contributions:
Abdurrahman ibn Awf's compassion extended to those in need, as he played a pivotal role in the liberation of captives during the Battle of Uhud. He freed thirty captives and generously provided each with 1000 gold coins,

alleviating their suffering and restoring their freedom. Furthermore, his dedication to the defense of Islam was evident in his provision of 500 horses and 500 loaded camels for the Tabuk expedition, ensuring the readiness and mobility of the Muslim army.

Exemplary Acts of Charity:
Abdurrahman ibn Awf's acts of charity were legendary, earning him praise and admiration from both the Prophet Muhammad (peace be upon him) and his companions. On one occasion, upon his arrival in Medina with 700 camels laden with essential provisions, including wheat, flour, and various grains, the Prophet's wife, Aisha, remarked that he would enter Paradise in a state of utmost humility. In response to this commendation, Abdurrahman ibn Awf vowed to distribute all the camels and their loads in the way of Allah, a promise witnessed by Hazrat Aisha herself.

Legacy and Final Resting Place:
Abdurrahman ibn Awf's life of extraordinary generosity and service to Islam concluded in Madinah at the age of 75, in the year 651. As per his wishes, Hazrat Osman led his funeral prayer, marking the end of a life dedicated to the principles of charity, compassion, and selflessness. His legacy continues to inspire believers to emulate his example of generosity and devotion to the cause of Islam.

Abdul Rahman bin Auf's Wealth Evaluation
At the time of Abd al-Rahman ibn 'Awf's رضي الله عنه passing, his wealth, valued in gold coins, amounted to 3.1 billion Islamic dinars.

Given that 1 Islamic Dinar equals 4.25 grams of gold per coin, if we convert the entire wealth into USD, Abd Al-Rahman ibn 'Awf's رضي الله عنه net worth would be calculated as follows:

4.25 x 3,103,000,000 x 64 = USD 849 billion.

For perspective, Elon Musk currently holds the title of the world's richest person with a net worth of $210.2 billion, while Abd al-Rahman ibn 'Awf's net worth is estimated at $849 billion.

Abdul Rahman bin Auf's Estimated Net Worth
Upon the passing of Abd al-Rahman ibn 'Awf, his net worth, valued in gold coins, varied across sources, with figures ranging from $606 billion to $849 billion.

Given the conversion rate of 1 Islamic Dinar equating to 4.25 grams of gold per coin, the wealth estimation fluctuates depending on the source. Some accounts cite a total of $606 billion, while others suggest $769 billion or even $849 billion.

This discrepancy underscores the challenge of precisely determining historical wealth, with differing calculations and interpretations leading to varying conclusions. Regardless of the exact figure, Abd al-Rahman ibn 'Awf's substantial wealth is a testament to his success and influence during his lifetime.

Abdul-Rahman bin Awf: Father of Abdur-Rahman ibn Awf, Wealthy Merchant in Mecca

Abdul-Rahman bin Awf, a distinguished figure in early Islamic history, is celebrated for his role as a wealthy merchant in Mecca and as the father of Abdur-Rahman ibn Awf, a renowned companion of the Prophet Muhammad (ﷺ)(peace be upon him). Born into a prominent family in Mecca, Abdul-Rahman emerged as a prominent figure in the commercial and social fabric of the city, playing a pivotal role in trade and commerce. This comprehensive essay delves into the life, achievements, and legacy of Abdul-Rahman bin Awf, highlighting his prominence as a merchant, his contributions to the early Muslim community, and his enduring influence on Islamic history.

Early Life and Background:

Abdul-Rahman bin Awf was born into a noble and affluent family in Mecca, a city that served as the commercial and religious center of the Arabian Peninsula. Little is known about his early life, but it is believed that he grew up in a household known for its wealth, influence, and adherence to traditional Arab customs and values. From a young age, Abdul-Rahman demonstrated intelligence, resilience, and a keen interest in commerce, traits that would shape his future endeavors as a merchant and supporter of Islam.

Role as a Wealthy Merchant:

Abdul-Rahman bin Awf distinguished himself as a wealthy and successful merchant, engaging in trade and commerce to support himself and his family. His business ventures took him across the Arabian Peninsula, where he established commercial connections and traded in goods ranging from textiles to spices. Despite his success as a merchant, Abdul-Rahman remained humble and grounded, never allowing worldly pursuits to distract him from his spiritual obligations.

Contributions to Meccan Society:

As one of the wealthiest and most influential merchants in Mecca, Abdul-Rahman bin Awf played a significant role in the economic and social life of the city. He contributed to the prosperity and development of Meccan society through his commercial ventures, philanthropic activities, and support for public projects. Abdul-Rahman's generosity, benevolence, and commitment to the welfare of his community earned him the respect and admiration of his peers and fellow citizens.

Family Life and Parenting:

Abdul-Rahman bin Awf was known for his devotion to his family and his exemplary parenting skills. He instilled in his children the values of honesty, integrity, and hard work, preparing them to succeed in both worldly and spiritual endeavors. His son, Abdur-Rahman ibn Awf, would go on to become one of the most illustrious companions of the Prophet Muhammad, a testament to the values and principles instilled by his father.

Encounter with Islam:

Abdul-Rahman bin Awf's encounter with Islam occurred during the early years of the prophetic mission of Muhammad (ﷺ)(peace be upon him). Influenced by the message of monotheism, social justice, and moral righteousness preached by the Prophet, Abdul-Rahman embraced Islam with sincerity and conviction, becoming one of the early converts to the faith. His unwavering commitment to Islam and his close association with the Prophet Muhammad (ﷺ)earned him the esteemed title of "Abdul-Rahman the Faithful."

Contributions to the Early Muslim Community:

In addition to his role as a merchant, Abdul-Rahman bin Awf made significant contributions to the early Muslim community, serving as a trusted advisor, mediator, and benefactor among his fellow companions. He played a key role in resolving disputes, reconciling differences, and upholding the principles of justice and equity within the

Muslim community. Abdul-Rahman's impartiality, wisdom, and integrity made him a beloved and respected figure among his peers and contributed to the cohesion and stability of early Islamic society.

Legacy and Influence:

Abdul-Rahman bin Awf's legacy endures as a testament to the enduring values and principles of Islam, inspiring Muslims around the world to emulate his example of piety, generosity, and commitment to social justice. His contributions as a wealthy merchant, devoted family man, and respected member of the early Muslim community exemplify the highest ideals of faith, integrity, and service to humanity. Abdul-Rahman's life and legacy continue to serve as a source of inspiration and guidance for Muslims seeking to uphold the teachings of Islam in their daily lives.

Abdul-Rahman bin Awf, celebrated as a wealthy merchant, devoted family man, and respected member of the early Muslim community, occupies a revered place in Islamic history and tradition. His prominence as a merchant, contributions to Meccan society, exemplary parenting skills, and commitment to Islam exemplify the highest ideals of faith, integrity, and service to humanity. Abdul-Rahman's life and legacy continue to serve as a timeless testament to the enduring values and principles of Islam, inspiring Muslims around the world to emulate his example and strive for excellence in all aspects of life.

Sayyiduna Abdullah Bin Umar رَضِیَ اللّٰهُ عَنْهُما

Sayyiduna Abdullah bin Umar bin al-Khattab (may Allah be pleased with him) was more than just a knowledgeable jurist and devout follower of the Prophet's Sunnah. He was also a skilled tradesman whose business practices were deeply influenced by the principles of Islam. With his unparalleled dedication to both spirituality and worldly affairs, he left a lasting legacy that continues to inspire Muslims around the world. *(Tabaqat Ibn-e-Sa'd, vol. 4, p. 111; Ajmal Tarjamah Akmal, p. 52; Faizan-e-Farooq-e-A'zam, vol. 1, p. 85)*

In his capacity as a proficient businessman, he engaged in various financial endeavors, including the trade of camels. It is recorded that he would participate in the camel market, which eventually evolved into the renowned al-Baqi Cemetery of Madinah. Through his astute dealings and ethical conduct, Sayyiduna Abdullah bin Umar (may Allah be pleased with him) exemplified the principles of honesty and integrity in commerce. *(Musnad Abi Dawood-lil-Tayalisi, p. 255, Hadith 1868; Lam'aat Al-Tanqih, vol. 5, p. 573, under the Hadith 2871).*

In addition to trading camels, Sayyiduna Abdullah bin Umar (may Allah be pleased with him) ventured into importing foreign goods. During the reign of his father, Sayyiduna Umar al-Farooq (may Allah be pleased with him), he and his brother, Sayyiduna Ubaydullah bin Umar (may Allah be pleased with him), undertook a journey to Iraq to acquire goods for trade. Upon their return to Madinah Munawwarah, they successfully sold these imported goods, showcasing their acumen in navigating international commerce and contributing to the economic prosperity of their community. *(Muwattta Imam Malik, vol. 2, p. 213, Raqm 1434)*.

Partnerships played a significant role in the business ventures of Sayyiduna Zuhrah bin Ma'bad (may Allah have mercy on him), who was the grandson of the esteemed companion Sayyiduna Abdullah bin Hisham (may Allah be pleased with him). Recalling his experiences, he shared that his grandfather would often take him to the marketplace to purchase grains. On these occasions, Sayyiduna Abdullah bin Umar and Sayyiduna Abdullah bin al-Zubayr (may Allah be pleased with them) would approach him and express their desire to become partners in his business. Their request was motivated by the blessings bestowed upon Sayyiduna Zuhrah bin Ma'bad by the Prophet Muhammad (peace be upon him). Recognizing the significance of this opportunity, Sayyiduna Zuhrah bin Ma'bad readily accepted them as partners in his business endeavors, illustrating the importance of cooperation and mutual support in the entrepreneurial pursuits of the early Muslim community. *(Bukhari, vol. 2, p. 145, Hadith 2501-2502; Usd-ul-Ghaabah, vol. 3, p. 421).*

An intriguing aspect of Sayyiduna Abdullah bin Umar's life was his extensive knowledge of trade laws and ethics, reflected in the numerous Hadith he narrated on the subject. His deep understanding of Islamic principles guided his business practices, as he frequently sought guidance from the Beloved Prophet Muhammad (peace be upon him) to ensure compliance with Islamic regulations. This commitment to upholding ethical standards in his commercial dealings underscores the importance of aligning business activities with the teachings of Islam, highlighting Sayyiduna Abdullah bin Umar's exemplary character and dedication to ethical conduct in all aspects of life.

- Sayyiduna Abdullah bin Umar was the recipient of a heartfelt prayer for blessings and goodness from the Beloved Prophet Muhammad (peace be upon him) during his childhood.

- A mudarabah is a business partnership characterized by one party, the rabb-ul-mal, investing capital, while the other, the mudarib, invests labor. (Reference: Bahar-e-Shari'at, vol. 3, p. 1)

- Currency exchange, also known as forex trading, involves the swapping of one currency for another. This can include commodity money with intrinsic value, such as gold and silver, or fiat money, such as modern coins and banknotes. (Reference: Bahar-e-Shari'at, vol. 2, p. 14)

abu dharr al-ghifari trade in islamic history

In the secluded Waddan valley, nestled between Makkah and the outside world, resided the tribe of Ghifar, also known as Banu Ghafir. Their existence revolved around the meager provisions brought by the trade caravans of the Quraysh, which traversed the route between Syria and Makkah. However, it is believed that the Ghifar supplemented their livelihood by occasionally resorting to raiding these caravans when their needs were not adequately met.

Among the members of this tribe was Jundub ibn Junadah, affectionately known as Abu Dharr. He holds the distinction of being the fourth or fifth individual to embrace Islam, signifying his early recognition of the message brought by the Prophet Muhammad (peace be upon him). Prior to his conversion, little is documented about Abu Dharr's life, leaving much of his pre-Islamic journey shrouded in mystery.

Narrated by Abdullah bin Amr (R.A.) that the Messenger of Allah (S.A.W.) said:

"There is no one more truthful, that the sky has shaded and the earth has carried, than Abu Dharr." (Tirmidhi: 3801)

Renowned for his courage, composure, and foresight, Abu Dharr (may Allah be pleased with him) was also distinguished by his disdain for the idolatrous practices prevalent among his people. Rejecting the absurd religious beliefs and the pervasive corruption within Arab society, he yearned for a transformative change that would steer his community away from the shadows of superstition.

Amidst the desolate expanse of the Waddan desert, word reached Abu Dharr (may Allah be pleased with him) of a new Prophet (peace be upon him) who had emerged in Makkah. Filled with hope that the Prophet's arrival would herald a shift in the hearts and minds of the people, guiding them towards enlightenment, Abu Dharr wasted no time in summoning his brother, Anees, to discuss this momentous development.

Abbas ibn Abd al-Muttalib: Uncle of Prophet Muhammad (ﷺ)(PBUH), Businessman, and Convert to Islam

Abbas ibn Abd al-Muttalib, a significant figure in Islamic history, is known for his role as the uncle of Prophet Muhammad (ﷺ)(peace be upon him), his prowess as a businessman, and his eventual conversion to Islam. Born into the prestigious Banu Hashim clan of the Quraysh tribe in Mecca, Abbas played a pivotal role in the early years of Islam and contributed to the growth and development of the Muslim community. This comprehensive essay explores the life, achievements, and legacy of Abbas ibn Abd al-

Muttalib, highlighting his familial ties to the Prophet Muhammad, his business acumen, and his journey to embracing Islam.

Early Life and Family Background:

Abbas ibn Abd al-Muttalib was born into the noble Banu Hashim clan of the Quraysh tribe in Mecca, a lineage renowned for its honor, nobility, and leadership. He was the son of Abd al-Muttalib, making him the paternal uncle of Prophet Muhammad (ﷺ)(peace be upon him). From a young age, Abbas was raised in a household known for its piety, generosity, and influence in Meccan society. His familial ties to the Prophet Muhammad (ﷺ)would later play a significant role in his journey to Islam.

Role as a Businessman:

Abbas ibn Abd al-Muttalib distinguished himself as a successful and astute businessman, engaging in trade and commerce across the Arabian Peninsula. His business ventures brought him wealth, prestige, and influence in Meccan society, and he became known as one of the wealthiest merchants in the region. Abbas's keen business acumen, shrewd negotiations, and commitment to fair dealings earned him respect and admiration among his peers and competitors.

Early Opposition to Islam:

Despite his familial ties to the Prophet Muhammad, Abbas initially opposed Islam along with other members of the Quraysh tribe. Like many of his contemporaries, Abbas was wary of the revolutionary message preached by his nephew and feared the potential disruption it could bring to the established order in Mecca. He resisted the call to Islam and remained skeptical of its teachings, preferring to maintain the status quo and protect the interests of his community and business associates.

Encounter with Islam:

Abbas ibn Abd al-Muttalib's perspective on Islam began to change after witnessing the unwavering conviction and moral integrity of the early Muslims, including his own nephew, Prophet Muhammad. He was deeply impressed by the character and conduct of the Muslims, who demonstrated compassion, humility, and a commitment to social justice. Abbas's curiosity about Islam grew, and he began to question his previous opposition to the faith, eventually leading to his gradual acceptance and eventual conversion to Islam.

Conversion to Islam:

Abbas ibn Abd al-Muttalib's conversion to Islam was a pivotal moment in his life and in the history of the Muslim community. After years of hesitation and uncertainty, Abbas finally embraced Islam and pledged allegiance to the Prophet Muhammad, affirming his belief in the oneness of God and the prophethood of Muhammad. His conversion was met with joy and celebration among the Muslims, who welcomed him into the fold of Islam with open arms and hearts.

Role in the Muslim Community:

Following his conversion to Islam, Abbas ibn Abd al-Muttalib played an active role in the Muslim community, supporting the Prophet Muhammad (ﷺ)and contributing to the growth and development of the nascent Islamic state. He used his wealth, influence, and connections to help the Muslims navigate the challenges they faced in Mecca and later in Medina. Abbas's unwavering support and dedication to Islam earned him the respect and admiration of his fellow companions and successors.

Legacy and Influence:

Abbas ibn Abd al-Muttalib's legacy endures as a testament to the transformative power of faith and the capacity for personal growth and change. His journey from initial opposition to eventual acceptance of Islam serves as a powerful example of spiritual transformation and redemption. Abbas's conversion to Islam also highlights the importance of familial ties and personal relationships in the spread of the faith, as his connection to the Prophet Muhammad (ﷺ)played a crucial role in his journey to Islam.

Abbas ibn Abd al-Muttalib, celebrated as the uncle of Prophet Muhammad (ﷺ)and a successful businessman, occupies a revered place in Islamic history and tradition. His journey from initial opposition to eventual acceptance of Islam exemplifies the transformative power of faith and the capacity for personal growth and change. Abbas's conversion to Islam and his subsequent contributions to the Muslim community serve as a timeless testament to the enduring values of faith, resilience, and spiritual enlightenment. His legacy continues to inspire Muslims around the world to embrace the teachings of Islam and strive for excellence in all aspects of life.

Safwan ibn Umayyah: From Rivalry to Embrace - The Journey of a Wealthy Merchant with the Prophet Muhammad (ﷺ)(PBUH)

Safwan ibn Umayyah, a prominent figure in early Islamic history, is known for his transformation from a wealthy merchant and rival of the Prophet Muhammad (ﷺ)(peace be upon him) before Islam to a devoted follower of the Islamic faith. Born into the prestigious Umayyah clan of the Quraysh tribe in Mecca, Safwan's life journey is a remarkable tale of spiritual awakening, humility, and redemption. This comprehensive essay delves into the life, achievements, and transformation of Safwan ibn Umayyah, highlighting his role as a wealthy merchant, his initial opposition to Islam, and his eventual embrace of the faith.

Early Life and Background:

Safwan ibn Umayyah was born into the influential
Umayyah clan of the Quraysh tribe in Mecca, a city
renowned for its commercial and religious significance.
Little is known about his early life, but it is believed that he
grew up in a household known for its wealth, power, and
influence. Safwan inherited his family's business acumen
and entrepreneurial spirit, laying the foundation for his
future success as a merchant and leader in Meccan society.

Role as a Wealthy Merchant:

Safwan ibn Umayyah distinguished himself as a wealthy
and successful merchant, engaging in trade and commerce
to expand his family's wealth and influence. His business
ventures took him across the Arabian Peninsula, where he
established commercial connections and traded in goods
ranging from textiles to spices. Safwan's keen business
sense, astute negotiations, and strategic investments earned
him a reputation as one of the most prominent merchants in
Mecca, cementing his position in the city's elite circles.

Rivalry with the Prophet Muhammad (ﷺ)(PBUH):

Prior to his embrace of Islam, Safwan ibn Umayyah was
among the staunch opponents of the Prophet Muhammad
(ﷺ)and the burgeoning Islamic movement in Mecca.
Like many members of the Quraysh tribe, Safwan viewed

Islam as a threat to the traditional religious and social order of Meccan society. He actively opposed the message of monotheism preached by the Prophet, fearing that it would undermine his own status and influence in the community.

Encounter with Islam:

Safwan ibn Umayyah's encounter with Islam occurred during the early years of the prophetic mission of Muhammad (ﷺ)(peace be upon him). Despite his initial opposition to Islam, Safwan's heart was touched by the beauty and truth of the Quranic message, leading him to reconsider his stance towards the new faith. After witnessing the patience, humility, and integrity of the Prophet Muhammad, Safwan began to question his own beliefs and priorities, eventually leading to his embrace of Islam.

Transformation and Embrace of Islam:

Safwan ibn Umayyah's transformation from a staunch opponent of Islam to a devoted follower of the faith is a testament to the power of spiritual awakening and divine guidance. Over time, Safwan's heart softened towards the teachings of Islam, and he recognized the truth of the message brought by the Prophet Muhammad. With humility and sincerity, Safwan embraced Islam, seeking forgiveness for his past opposition and striving to live according to the principles of faith, compassion, and justice.

Contributions to the Muslim Community:

After embracing Islam, Safwan ibn Umayyah became a devoted follower of the Prophet Muhammad (ﷺ)and an active participant in the Muslim community. He used his wealth, influence, and leadership skills to support the cause of Islam, contributing generously to charitable causes, sponsoring needy Muslims, and advocating for justice and equality within society. Safwan's transformation from a wealthy merchant to a compassionate servant of God exemplifies the transformative power of faith and the capacity for redemption in Islam.

Legacy and Influence:

Safwan ibn Umayyah's journey from rivalry to embrace serves as a powerful example of the transformative power of faith and the capacity for redemption in Islam. His humility, sincerity, and devotion to Islam earned him the respect and admiration of his fellow Muslims, and his story continues to inspire believers around the world to seek forgiveness, embrace change, and strive for righteousness in their lives. Safwan's legacy endures as a testament to the transformative power of faith and the boundless mercy of God.

Safwan ibn Umayyah's journey from rivalry to embrace is a powerful testament to the transformative power of faith and the capacity for redemption in Islam. His transformation from a wealthy merchant and rival of the Prophet

Muhammad (ﷺ)to a devoted follower of the Islamic faith serves as an inspiring example of the transformative power of faith and the boundless mercy of God. Safwan's story reminds us that no one is beyond the reach of divine guidance and forgiveness, and that true success lies in embracing the truth and living according to the principles of faith, compassion, and justice.

Safwan ibn Umayyah: From Rivalry to Embrace - The Journey of a Wealthy Merchant with the Prophet Muhammad (ﷺ)(PBUH)

Safwan ibn Umayyah, a prominent figure in early Islamic history, is known for his transformation from a wealthy merchant and rival of the Prophet Muhammad (ﷺ)(peace be upon him) before Islam to a devoted follower of the Islamic faith. Born into the prestigious Umayyah clan of the Quraysh tribe in Mecca, Safwan's life journey is a remarkable tale of spiritual awakening, humility, and redemption. This comprehensive essay delves into the life, achievements, and transformation of Safwan ibn Umayyah, highlighting his role as a wealthy merchant, his initial opposition to Islam, and his eventual embrace of the faith.

Early Life and Background:

Safwan ibn Umayyah was born into the influential Umayyah clan of the Quraysh tribe in Mecca, a city renowned for its commercial and religious significance. Little is known about his early life, but it is believed that he grew up in a household known for its wealth, power, and influence. Safwan inherited his family's business acumen and entrepreneurial spirit, laying the foundation for his future success as a merchant and leader in Meccan society.

Role as a Wealthy Merchant:

Safwan ibn Umayyah distinguished himself as a wealthy and successful merchant, engaging in trade and commerce to expand his family's wealth and influence. His business ventures took him across the Arabian Peninsula, where he established commercial connections and traded in goods ranging from textiles to spices. Safwan's keen business sense, astute negotiations, and strategic investments earned him a reputation as one of the most prominent merchants in Mecca, cementing his position in the city's elite circles.

Rivalry with the Prophet Muhammad (ﷺ)(PBUH):

Prior to his embrace of Islam, Safwan ibn Umayyah was among the staunch opponents of the Prophet Muhammad (ﷺ)and the burgeoning Islamic movement in Mecca. Like many members of the Quraysh tribe, Safwan viewed Islam as a threat to the traditional religious and social order of Meccan society. He actively opposed the message of monotheism preached by the Prophet, fearing that it would undermine his own status and influence in the community.

Encounter with Islam:

Safwan ibn Umayyah's encounter with Islam occurred during the early years of the prophetic mission of Muhammad (ﷺ)(peace be upon him). Despite his initial opposition to Islam, Safwan's heart was touched by the beauty and truth of the Quranic message, leading him to reconsider his stance towards the new faith. After witnessing the patience, humility, and integrity of the Prophet Muhammad, Safwan began to question his own beliefs and priorities, eventually leading to his embrace of Islam.

Transformation and Embrace of Islam:

Safwan ibn Umayyah's transformation from a staunch opponent of Islam to a devoted follower of the faith is a testament to the power of spiritual awakening and divine guidance. Over time, Safwan's heart softened towards the teachings of Islam, and he recognized the truth of the message brought by the Prophet Muhammad. With humility and sincerity, Safwan embraced Islam, seeking forgiveness for his past opposition and striving to live according to the principles of faith, compassion, and justice.

Contributions to the Muslim Community:

After embracing Islam, Safwan ibn Umayyah became a devoted follower of the Prophet Muhammad (ﷺ)and an active participant in the Muslim community. He used his wealth, influence, and leadership skills to support the cause of Islam, contributing generously to charitable causes, sponsoring needy Muslims, and advocating for justice and equality within society. Safwan's transformation from a wealthy merchant to a compassionate servant of God exemplifies the transformative power of faith and the capacity for redemption in Islam.

Legacy and Influence:

Safwan ibn Umayyah's journey from rivalry to embrace serves as a powerful example of the transformative power of faith and the capacity for redemption in Islam. His humility, sincerity, and devotion to Islam earned him the respect and admiration of his fellow Muslims, and his story continues to inspire believers around the world to seek forgiveness, embrace change, and strive for righteousness in their lives. Safwan's legacy endures as a testament to the transformative power of faith and the boundless mercy of God.

Safwan ibn Umayyah's journey from rivalry to embrace is a powerful testament to the transformative power of faith and the capacity for redemption in Islam. His transformation from a wealthy merchant and rival of the Prophet Muhammad (ﷺ)to a devoted follower of the Islamic faith serves as an inspiring example of the transformative power of faith and the boundless mercy of God. Safwan's story reminds us that no one is beyond the reach of divine guidance and forgiveness, and that true success lies in embracing the truth and living according to the principles of faith, compassion, and justice.

Hakim ibn Hizam: The Late Convert - A Wealthy Merchant's Journey to Islam

Hakim ibn Hizam, a significant figure in early Islamic history, is notable for his late embrace of Islam despite being a wealthy merchant in Mecca. Born into a respected family in the Quraysh tribe, Hakim grew up amidst the bustling commercial and religious activity of pre-Islamic Arabia. This essay explores the life, achievements, and spiritual journey of Hakim ibn Hizam, shedding light on his wealth, his encounters with Islam, and the circumstances surrounding his late conversion to the faith.

Early Life and Background:

Hakim ibn Hizam was born into the prestigious Hizam clan of the Quraysh tribe in Mecca, a city renowned for its commercial and religious significance. From a young age, Hakim was exposed to the intricacies of trade and commerce, as his family was involved in various business ventures. Despite his privileged upbringing, Hakim was known for his humility, generosity, and keen sense of integrity, qualities that would shape his later life and interactions with the Islamic faith.

Role as a Wealthy Merchant:

As he matured, Hakim ibn Hizam distinguished himself as a wealthy and astute merchant, engaging in trade and commerce to expand his family's wealth and influence. His business ventures took him across the Arabian Peninsula, where he established lucrative commercial connections and traded in goods ranging from textiles to spices. Hakim's shrewd business acumen and ethical conduct earned him a reputation as one of the most successful merchants in Mecca, consolidating his position within the city's elite circles.

Encounters with Islam:

Despite his prominence as a wealthy merchant, Hakim ibn Hizam initially remained aloof from the emerging Islamic movement in Mecca. He was among the Quraysh elites who viewed Islam with skepticism and apprehension, fearing that its spread would undermine their traditional power structures and social order. However, as Islam gained momentum and followers in Mecca, Hakim's curiosity about the teachings of the faith began to grow, leading to a series of profound encounters that would eventually shape his spiritual journey.

Late Conversion to Islam:

Unlike many of his contemporaries, Hakim ibn Hizam's embrace of Islam came relatively late in life. Despite his initial reservations, Hakim was deeply moved by the sincerity, humility, and moral integrity of the Prophet Muhammad (ﷺ)(peace be upon him) and his companions. Over time, Hakim's heart softened towards the message of Islam, and he began to recognize the truth and beauty of its teachings. Eventually, in a moment of spiritual clarity, Hakim embraced Islam, seeking forgiveness for his past indifference and pledging allegiance to God and His Messenger.

Contributions to the Muslim Community:

Following his conversion to Islam, Hakim ibn Hizam became an active and dedicated member of the Muslim community, using his wealth, influence, and business acumen to support the cause of Islam. He contributed generously to charitable causes, sponsored needy Muslims, and played a role in the propagation and dissemination of Islamic knowledge. Despite his late entry into the faith, Hakim's sincerity, devotion, and commitment to Islam earned him the respect and admiration of his fellow Muslims.

Legacy and Influence:

Hakim ibn Hizam's late conversion to Islam serves as a powerful reminder of the transformative power of faith and the capacity for spiritual growth and renewal. His journey from skepticism to belief, from indifference to devotion, underscores the universal nature of Islam's message and its ability to touch the hearts of people from all walks of life. Hakim's story continues to inspire believers around the world to embrace Islam with sincerity and humility, regardless of their background or circumstances.

Hakim ibn Hizam's late embrace of Islam is a testament to the transformative power of faith and the boundless mercy of God. His journey from skepticism to belief, from indifference to devotion, serves as a powerful reminder of the universal appeal of Islam's message and its ability to transform lives. Hakim's story is a source of inspiration and encouragement for believers seeking to deepen their faith and renew their commitment to Islam, regardless of the obstacles they may face along the way.

Ubaydah ibn al-Harith: A Merchant's Faith - The Journey of an Early Convert to Islam

Ubaydah ibn al-Harith, a significant figure in early Islamic history, is renowned for his dual role as a prominent merchant and an early convert to Islam. Born into a respected family in Mecca, Ubaydah's life journey is marked by his unwavering commitment to the Islamic faith and his contributions to the burgeoning Muslim community. This essay explores the life, achievements, and legacy of Ubaydah ibn al-Harith, shedding light on his role as a merchant, his encounter with Islam, and his pivotal role in the early Islamic movement.

Early Life and Background:

Ubaydah ibn al-Harith was born into a noble and affluent family in Mecca, a city that served as the commercial and religious center of the Arabian Peninsula. From a young age, Ubaydah was exposed to the intricacies of trade and commerce, as his family was involved in various business ventures. Despite his privileged upbringing, Ubaydah was known for his humility, generosity, and keen sense of integrity, qualities that would shape his later interactions with the Islamic faith.

Role as a Prominent Merchant:

As he matured, Ubaydah ibn al-Harith emerged as a successful and respected merchant, engaging in trade and commerce to expand his family's wealth and influence. His business ventures took him across the Arabian Peninsula, where he established lucrative commercial connections and traded in goods ranging from textiles to spices. Ubaydah's keen business acumen, ethical conduct, and commitment to fair trade earned him a reputation as one of the most prominent merchants in Mecca, solidifying his position within the city's elite circles.

Encounter with Islam:

Ubaydah ibn al-Harith's encounter with Islam occurred during the early years of the prophetic mission of Muhammad (ﷺ)(peace be upon him). Influenced by the sincerity, humility, and moral integrity of the Prophet Muhammad (ﷺ)and his companions, Ubaydah was drawn to the message of monotheism, social justice, and moral righteousness preached by Islam. Despite facing opposition and persecution from the Quraysh elite, Ubaydah's heart was touched by the truth and beauty of the Quranic message, leading him to embrace Islam with sincerity and conviction.

Early Conversion to Islam:

Unlike many of his contemporaries, Ubaydah ibn al-Harith was among the early converts to Islam, recognizing the truth of the faith and pledging allegiance to God and His Messenger at a time when the Muslim community was still in its infancy. His unwavering commitment to Islam and his willingness to endure persecution and hardship for the sake of his faith earned him the admiration and respect of the Prophet Muhammad (ﷺ)and his fellow companions.

Contributions to the Muslim Community:

Following his conversion to Islam, Ubaydah ibn al-Harith became an active and dedicated member of the Muslim community, using his wealth, influence, and leadership skills to support the cause of Islam. He contributed generously to charitable causes, sponsored needy Muslims, and played a key role in the propagation and dissemination of Islamic knowledge. Ubaydah's sincerity, devotion, and commitment to Islam made him a beloved and respected figure among his peers and earned him a prominent place in the annals of Islamic history.

Legacy and Influence:

Ubaydah ibn al-Harith's legacy endures as a testament to the transformative power of faith and the capacity for spiritual growth and renewal. His early conversion to Islam, unwavering commitment to the faith, and contributions to the Muslim community serve as an inspiring example for believers seeking to deepen their faith and live according to the principles of Islam. Ubaydah's story continues to inspire Muslims around the world to embrace Islam with sincerity and conviction, regardless of the challenges they may face along the way.

Ubaydah ibn al-Harith's journey from a prominent merchant to an early convert to Islam is a powerful testament to the transformative power of faith and the boundless mercy of God. His unwavering commitment to Islam, despite facing persecution and hardship, serves as an inspiring example for believers seeking to deepen their faith and live according to the principles of Islam. Ubaydah's story continues to inspire Muslims around the world to embrace Islam with sincerity and conviction, regardless of the obstacles they may encounter on their spiritual journey.

Suhayb ar-Rumi: The Journey of a Trader from Byzantine Territory to Medina

Suhayb ar-Rumi, a prominent figure in early Islamic history, is celebrated for his remarkable journey as a trader from Byzantine territory to the city of Medina. Born into a prosperous family in the Byzantine Empire, Suhayb's life took a dramatic turn when he embraced Islam and migrated to Medina, where he became known for his piety, wisdom, and dedication to the Prophet Muhammad (ﷺ)(peace be upon him). This essay delves into the life, achievements, and legacy of Suhayb ar-Rumi, shedding light on his background as a trader, his conversion to Islam, and his pivotal role in the early Muslim community.

Early Life and Background:

Suhayb ar-Rumi was born into a wealthy and influential family in the Byzantine Empire, a region characterized by its rich cultural heritage and strategic significance as a center of trade and commerce. Little is known about Suhayb's early life, but it is believed that he received a privileged upbringing and was exposed to the intricacies of trade and commerce from a young age. Despite his affluent background, Suhayb was known for his intelligence, humility, and strong sense of moral integrity, qualities that would shape his later life and interactions with the Islamic faith.

Role as a Trader:

As he matured, Suhayb ar-Rumi emerged as a skilled and enterprising trader, engaging in commerce across the Byzantine Empire and beyond. His business ventures took him to various regions of the Mediterranean, where he established lucrative commercial connections and traded in goods ranging from textiles to precious metals. Suhayb's keen business acumen, ethical conduct, and commitment to fair trade earned him a reputation as one of the most successful traders in the region, solidifying his position within the merchant elite.

Encounter with Islam:

Suhayb ar-Rumi's encounter with Islam occurred during the early years of the prophetic mission of Muhammad (ﷺ)(peace be upon him). Influenced by the sincerity, humility, and moral integrity of the Prophet Muhammad (ﷺ)and his companions, Suhayb was drawn to the message of monotheism, social justice, and moral righteousness preached by Islam. Despite facing opposition and persecution from the Byzantine authorities, Suhayb's heart was touched by the truth and beauty of the Quranic message, leading him to embrace Islam with sincerity and conviction.

Migration to Medina:

Faced with increasing hostility and persecution in Byzantine territory due to his newfound faith, Suhayb ar-

Rumi made the courageous decision to migrate to the city of Medina, where the Muslim community was establishing a fledgling state under the leadership of the Prophet Muhammad. Despite the challenges and dangers posed by the arduous journey, Suhayb's unwavering faith and determination guided him safely to his destination, where he was warmly welcomed by the Prophet and his companions.

Contributions to the Muslim Community:

Following his migration to Medina, Suhayb ar-Rumi became an integral member of the Muslim community, using his wealth, influence, and expertise to support the cause of Islam. He contributed generously to charitable causes, sponsored needy Muslims, and played a key role in the defense and expansion of the Muslim state. Suhayb's sincerity, devotion, and commitment to Islam earned him the respect and admiration of his fellow companions, who regarded him as a trusted advisor and confidant.

Legacy and Influence:

Suhayb ar-Rumi's legacy endures as a testament to the transformative power of faith and the resilience of the human spirit. His remarkable journey from Byzantine territory to the city of Medina exemplifies the courage, determination, and sacrifice of early Muslims who embraced Islam in the face of adversity. Suhayb's story continues to inspire Muslims around the world to remain steadfast in their faith and to uphold the values of integrity, compassion, and justice in all aspects of their lives.

Suhayb ar-Rumi's journey from trader in Byzantine territory to esteemed member of the Muslim community in Medina is a testament to the transformative power of faith and the resilience of the human spirit. His unwavering commitment to Islam, despite facing persecution and hardship, serves as an inspiring example for believers seeking to navigate the challenges of the modern world with courage, integrity, and compassion. Suhayb's legacy continues to inspire Muslims around the world to embrace the teachings of Islam and to strive for excellence in all aspects of their lives.

Hudhayfah ibn Yaman: The Intelligent Companion of the Prophet Muhammad (ﷺ)(PBUH)

Hudhayfah ibn Yaman occupies a distinguished place in Islamic history as a trusted companion of the Prophet Muhammad (ﷺ)(peace be upon him) renowned for his intelligence, loyalty, and expertise in gathering information. Born into the Yaman clan of the Quraysh tribe in Mecca, Hudhayfah's life journey is marked by his unwavering commitment to Islam and his pivotal role in supporting the Prophet Muhammad (ﷺ)during times of trial and tribulation. This essay explores the life, achievements, and legacy of Hudhayfah ibn Yaman, shedding light on his background as a merchant, his close association with the Prophet Muhammad, and his contributions to the early Muslim community.

Early Life and Background:

Hudhayfah ibn Yaman was born into the Yaman clan of the Quraysh tribe in Mecca, a city renowned for its commercial and religious significance. Little is known about his early life, but it is believed that he grew up in a household known for its piety, integrity, and adherence to traditional Arab customs and values. From a young age, Hudhayfah demonstrated intelligence, resilience, and a keen interest in commerce, traits that would shape his future endeavors as a merchant and supporter of Islam.

Role as a Merchant:

As he matured, Hudhayfah ibn Yaman emerged as a successful and respected merchant, engaging in trade and commerce to support himself and his family. His business ventures took him across the Arabian Peninsula, where he established commercial connections and traded in goods ranging from textiles to spices. Despite his success as a merchant, Hudhayfah remained humble and grounded, never allowing worldly pursuits to distract him from his spiritual obligations.

Encounter with Islam:

Hudhayfah ibn Yaman's encounter with Islam occurred during the early years of the prophetic mission of

Muhammad (ﷺ)(peace be upon him). Influenced by the sincerity, humility, and moral integrity of the Prophet Muhammad (ﷺ)and his companions, Hudhayfah was drawn to the message of monotheism, social justice, and moral righteousness preached by Islam. He embraced Islam with sincerity and conviction, becoming one of the early converts to the faith.

Role as a Companion of the Prophet:

Hudhayfah ibn Yaman distinguished himself as a loyal and devoted companion of the Prophet Muhammad, accompanying him on various expeditions, campaigns, and diplomatic missions. Known for his intelligence, keen observation, and attention to detail, Hudhayfah played a crucial role in gathering information and intelligence for the Muslim community, helping to ensure its safety and security in the face of external threats and internal challenges.

Contributions to the Muslim Community:

In addition to his role as a merchant and companion of the Prophet, Hudhayfah ibn Yaman made significant contributions to the Muslim community, serving as a trusted advisor, mediator, and confidant among his fellow companions. He played a key role in resolving disputes, reconciling differences, and upholding the principles of justice and equity within the Muslim community. Hudhayfah's intelligence, wisdom, and integrity made him a beloved and respected figure among his peers and contributed to the cohesion and stability of early Islamic society.

Legacy and Influence:

Hudhayfah ibn Yaman's legacy endures as a testament to the enduring values and principles of Islam, inspiring Muslims around the world to emulate his example of piety, resilience, and commitment to social justice. His contributions as a merchant, companion of the Prophet, and trusted advisor exemplify the highest ideals of faith, integrity, and service to humanity. Hudhayfah's life and legacy continue to serve as a source of inspiration and guidance for Muslims seeking to uphold the teachings of Islam in their daily lives.

Hudhayfah ibn Yaman, celebrated as a merchant, companion of the Prophet Muhammad, and trusted advisor, occupies a revered place in Islamic history and tradition. His intelligence, loyalty, and dedication to Islam exemplify the highest ideals of faith, resilience, and devotion to God. Hudhayfah's contributions to the Muslim community and his unwavering commitment to the principles of justice and equity serve as a timeless testament to the enduring values of Islam, inspiring Muslims around the world to emulate his example and strive for excellence in all aspects of life.

Thaabit ibn Qays: The Generous Companion of the Prophet Muhammad (ﷺ)(PBUH)

Thaabit ibn Qays stands out in Islamic history as a notable companion of the Prophet Muhammad (ﷺ)(peace be upon him), celebrated for his remarkable generosity, compassion, and unwavering support for the nascent Muslim community. As a merchant by trade, Thaabit's life journey was intertwined with the pursuit of commerce and the principles of charity and kindness. This essay aims to explore the life, contributions, and legacy of Thaabit ibn Qays, shedding light on his role as a merchant, his association with the Prophet Muhammad, and his exemplary generosity towards others.

Early Life and Background:

Thaabit ibn Qays was born into a noble and respected family in pre-Islamic Arabia, where trade and commerce played a pivotal role in society. Little is known about his early life, but it is believed that he received a traditional upbringing steeped in the values of honor, integrity, and compassion. From a young age, Thaabit demonstrated a natural inclination towards generosity and kindness, traits that would define his character in later years.

Role as a Merchant:

Thaabit ibn Qays pursued a career as a merchant, engaging in trade and commerce to support himself and his family. His business ventures took him across the Arabian Peninsula, where he traded in goods ranging from textiles to spices, establishing himself as a successful and respected merchant. Despite his commercial success, Thaabit never allowed his wealth to overshadow his commitment to charity and helping those in need.

Encounter with Islam:

Thaabit ibn Qays's encounter with Islam occurred during the early years of the prophetic mission of Muhammad (ﷺ)(peace be upon him). Influenced by the sincerity, compassion, and moral integrity of the Prophet Muhammad (ﷺ)and his companions, Thaabit was drawn to the message of monotheism, social justice, and moral righteousness preached by Islam. He embraced Islam wholeheartedly, recognizing it as the path to spiritual fulfillment and societal reform.

Role as a Companion of the Prophet:

Thaabit ibn Qays became a devoted companion of the Prophet Muhammad, accompanying him on various expeditions, campaigns, and diplomatic missions. Known for his generosity and compassion, Thaabit played a vital role in supporting the Muslim community, especially during times of hardship and adversity. He used his wealth and resources to provide for the needs of his fellow companions and to alleviate the suffering of the less fortunate.

Exemplary Generosity:

Thaabit ibn Qays's generosity was legendary among his contemporaries, earning him the admiration and respect of the Prophet Muhammad (ﷺ) and his fellow companions. He was known for his willingness to give generously to those in need, regardless of their social status or background. Thaabit's acts of charity and kindness touched the lives of countless individuals, leaving a lasting impact on the early Muslim community.

Legacy and Influence:

Thaabit ibn Qays's legacy endures as a testament to the transformative power of generosity and compassion. His exemplary life serves as an inspiration for Muslims around the world to emulate his example of selflessness and kindness towards others. Thaabit's commitment to charity and social justice embodies the highest ideals of Islam, reminding believers of their duty to care for the less fortunate and uphold the principles of compassion and empathy in all aspects of life.

Thaabit ibn Qays, celebrated as a merchant, companion of the Prophet Muhammad, and paragon of generosity, leaves behind a legacy of compassion and kindness that continues to inspire Muslims to this day. His unwavering commitment to helping others, regardless of personal cost, serves as a timeless reminder of the importance of generosity and empathy in Islam. Thaabit's life exemplifies the transformative power of charity and compassion, reminding believers of their duty to strive for excellence in character and conduct, following in the footsteps of the Prophet Muhammad (ﷺ)and his noble companions.

Jubair ibn Mut'im: The Late Conversion of a Wealthy Merchant to Islam

Jubair ibn Mut'im, a prominent figure in early Islamic history, is recognized for his late embrace of Islam despite being born into a wealthy and influential family in Mecca. His journey from affluence to faith highlights the transformative power of Islam and the capacity for spiritual growth and renewal. This essay aims to explore the life, circumstances, and significance of Jubair ibn Mut'im's conversion to Islam, shedding light on his background as a wealthy merchant, his encounter with the Islamic faith, and the impact of his decision on the early Muslim community.

Early Life and Background:

Jubair ibn Mut'im was born into the prestigious Mut'im clan of the Quraysh tribe in Mecca, a city renowned for its commercial and religious significance. Raised in a household of wealth and privilege, Jubair enjoyed the comforts and opportunities afforded by his affluent upbringing. As he matured, he became actively involved in the family's business ventures, engaging in trade and commerce to expand their wealth and influence.

Role as a Wealthy Merchant:

Jubair ibn Mut'im distinguished himself as a successful and respected merchant, engaging in trade across the Arabian Peninsula and beyond. His business ventures brought him prosperity and recognition within Meccan society, solidifying his position among the city's elite circles. Despite his material success, Jubair's heart remained restless, yearning for a deeper sense of purpose and meaning beyond the pursuit of wealth and worldly pleasures.

Encounter with Islam:

Jubair ibn Mut'im's encounter with Islam occurred during the early years of the prophetic mission of Muhammad (ﷺ)(peace be upon him). Initially skeptical of the new faith and its implications for Meccan society, Jubair viewed Islam with suspicion and apprehension, fearing that it would disrupt the existing social order and undermine his family's status and influence. However, as Islam gained momentum and followers in Mecca, Jubair's curiosity about the teachings of the faith began to grow, leading to a gradual shift in his perception and attitude towards Islam.

Late Conversion to Islam:

Unlike many of his contemporaries, Jubair ibn Mut'im's embrace of Islam came later in life, following a period of introspection and soul-searching. Despite his initial reservations, Jubair was deeply moved by the sincerity, humility, and moral integrity of the Prophet Muhammad

(ﷺ)and his companions. He recognized the truth and beauty of the Quranic message, and after much contemplation, he made the courageous decision to embrace Islam, seeking forgiveness for his past skepticism and opposition to the faith.

Impact on the Muslim Community:

Jubair ibn Mut'im's late conversion to Islam had a profound impact on the early Muslim community, serving as a testament to the transformative power of faith and the boundless mercy of God. His decision to embrace Islam despite the social and personal consequences demonstrated courage, humility, and a sincere desire for spiritual growth and renewal. Jubair's conversion also served to strengthen the Muslim community, inspiring others to reevaluate their own beliefs and priorities in light of the Quranic message.

Legacy and Influence:

Jubair ibn Mut'im's legacy endures as a testament to the transformative power of Islam and the capacity for spiritual growth and renewal. His late conversion to the faith serves as an inspiration for believers seeking to deepen their relationship with God and live according to the principles of Islam. Jubair's story reminds us that no one is beyond the reach of divine guidance and forgiveness, and that true success lies in submitting to the will of God and striving for righteousness in all aspects of life.

Jubair ibn Mut'im's late embrace of Islam serves as a powerful reminder of the transformative power of faith and the boundless mercy of God. His journey from skepticism to belief, from material wealth to spiritual fulfillment, underscores the universal appeal of Islam's message and its ability to transform lives. Jubair's story continues to inspire Muslims around the world to embrace Islam with sincerity and conviction, regardless of the obstacles they may face along the way, and to seek forgiveness and guidance from the One who is the source of all mercy and compassion.

Khadija bint Khuwaylid: The Exemplary Businesswoman and Beloved Wife of the Prophet Muhammad (ﷺ)(PBUH)

Khadija bint Khuwaylid holds a revered place in Islamic history as the first wife of the Prophet Muhammad (ﷺ)(peace be upon him) and a highly successful businesswoman in her own right. Her life story is a testament to the virtues of intelligence, courage, and compassion, as well as her pivotal role in supporting the early Muslim community. This essay aims to explore the remarkable life, achievements, and legacy of Khadija bint Khuwaylid, shedding light on her background as a businesswoman, her marriage to the Prophet Muhammad, and her enduring impact on Islam.

Early Life and Background:

Khadija bint Khuwaylid was born into the prestigious clan of Banu Asad in Mecca, a city known for its commercial and religious significance. From a young age, Khadija demonstrated exceptional intelligence, determination, and business acumen, traits that would distinguish her as one of the most successful entrepreneurs of her time. Despite being born into a noble family, Khadija's success in business was largely attributed to her own hard work, ingenuity, and perseverance.

Role as a Businesswoman:

Khadija bint Khuwaylid emerged as a highly successful businesswoman, engaging in trade and commerce across the Arabian Peninsula and beyond. Her business ventures involved the trading of goods such as textiles, spices, and precious metals, which brought her immense wealth and recognition within Meccan society. Khadija's keen business sense, integrity, and commitment to fair trade earned her a reputation as one of the most respected and influential merchants in Mecca.

Encounter with the Prophet Muhammad:

Khadija bint Khuwaylid first encountered the Prophet Muhammad (ﷺ)(peace be upon him) through her business dealings, as he was employed by her to oversee a trade caravan to Syria. Impressed by Muhammad's honesty, integrity, and moral character, Khadija developed a deep admiration and respect for him. Despite their age difference, Khadija was drawn to Muhammad's noble qualities and soon proposed marriage to him, an offer that Muhammad (ﷺ) accepted.

Marriage and Support of the Prophet:

Khadija bint Khuwaylid's marriage to the Prophet Muhammad (ﷺ) marked the beginning of a loving and supportive partnership that would endure throughout their lives. As Muhammad (ﷺ) embarked on his prophetic mission, Khadija stood by his side, offering unwavering support, encouragement, and guidance. She provided both emotional and financial support to Muhammad, enabling him to devote himself fully to spreading the message of Islam.

Legacy and Influence:

Khadija bint Khuwaylid's legacy as a pioneering business woman and devoted wife of the Prophet Muhammad (ﷺ) endures as a source of inspiration for Muslims around the world. Her remarkable achievements in the world of commerce serve as a testament to the capabilities and contributions of women in Islam. Khadija's unwavering support for the Prophet Muhammad (ﷺ) during the early years of Islam played a crucial role in the establishment and spread of the Muslim community.

Exemplary Traits:

Khadija bint Khuwaylid is remembered not only for her business acumen and wealth but also for her exemplary character and devotion to Islam. She embodied the values of compassion, generosity, and selflessness, setting a high standard for Muslims to emulate. Khadija's unwavering faith in God and her commitment to justice and righteousness serve as a timeless example for believers seeking to navigate the challenges of life with dignity and integrity.

Khadija bint Khuwaylid's life exemplifies the ideal of a successful businesswoman, devoted wife, and faithful servant of God. Her pioneering achievements in business and her unwavering support for the Prophet Muhammad (ﷺ)(peace be upon him) highlight the indispensable role of women in Islam and their capacity to make significant contributions to society. Khadija's legacy continues to inspire Muslims around the world to strive for excellence in all aspects of life and to uphold the values of integrity, compassion, and devotion to God.

Lubaba bint al-Harith: The Philanthropic Businesswoman of Quba Mosque

Lubaba bint al-Harith is a revered figure in Islamic history for her significant contributions as a businesswoman and philanthropist, particularly in the financing of the construction of the first mosque in Quba. Her life story exemplifies the intersection of commerce and piety, highlighting the profound impact that individual initiative and generosity can have on the development of religious institutions. This essay aims to delve into the remarkable life, achievements, and legacy of Lubaba bint al-Harith, shedding light on her background as a businesswoman, her philanthropic endeavors, and her enduring impact on the Muslim community.

Early Life and Background:

Lubaba bint al-Harith was born into a respected family in Medina, a city that would later become the epicenter of the Islamic world. Little is known about her early life, but it is believed that she grew up in an environment characterized by faith, integrity, and a strong sense of community. From a young age, Lubaba demonstrated a keen interest in commerce and entrepreneurship, traits that would serve her well in her later endeavors.

Role as a Businesswoman:

Lubaba bint al-Harith emerged as a successful and enterprising businesswoman, engaging in trade and commerce to support herself and her family. Her business ventures took her across the Arabian Peninsula, where she established lucrative commercial connections and traded in goods ranging from textiles to spices. Lubaba's keen business acumen, integrity, and commitment to fair trade earned her a reputation as one of the most respected and influential merchants in Medina.

Philanthropic Endeavors:

Lubaba bint al-Harith's most notable contribution came in the form of her generous financial support for the construction of the first mosque in Quba. Recognizing the importance of establishing a place of worship for the growing Muslim community, Lubaba generously donated her wealth to fund the construction of the mosque, ensuring that it would serve as a spiritual sanctuary and community center for generations to come. Her philanthropic gesture exemplified her deep devotion to Islam and her commitment to supporting the religious and social needs of her fellow Muslims.

Impact on the Muslim Community:

The construction of the Quba Mosque, made possible in part by Lubaba bint al-Harith's generous contributions, had a profound impact on the Muslim community of Medina and beyond. As the first mosque built by the Prophet Muhammad (ﷺ)(peace be upon him) upon his arrival in Medina, Quba Mosque served as a symbol of unity, piety, and community solidarity. It became a focal point for religious worship, education, and social interaction, fostering a sense of belonging and spiritual fulfillment among the early Muslim community.

Legacy and Influence:

Lubaba bint al-Harith's legacy endures as a testament to the transformative power of philanthropy and the enduring impact of individual initiative on the development of religious institutions. Her generous contributions to the construction of the Quba Mosque exemplify the values of compassion, generosity, and devotion to God that are central to the teachings of Islam. Lubaba's legacy continues to inspire Muslims around the world to emulate her example of selfless giving and to contribute to the betterment of their communities through acts of charity and kindness.

Lubaba bint al-Harith's life exemplifies the profound impact that individual initiative and generosity can have on the development of religious institutions and the welfare of the community. Her philanthropic contributions to the construction of the Quba Mosque serve as a timeless reminder of the importance of supporting religious and social initiatives that benefit society as a whole. Lubaba's legacy continues to inspire Muslims around the world to follow her example of selfless giving and to strive for excellence in all aspects of life, guided by the principles of compassion, integrity, and devotion to God.

Umm Salama: The Pious Wife and Resilient Trader of Prophet Muhammad (ﷺ)(PBUH)

Umm Salama holds a revered position in Islamic history as one of the wives of the Prophet Muhammad (ﷺ)(peace be upon him) and a remarkable example of resilience and devotion. Despite her esteemed role as a wife and mother, Umm Salama also continued her trading activities after embracing Islam, showcasing the compatibility of faith and worldly pursuits. This essay aims to explore the life, achievements, and legacy of Umm Salama, shedding light on her background as a trader, her marriage to the Prophet Muhammad, and her enduring impact on the Muslim community

Early Life and Background:

Umm Salama, whose original name was Hind bint Abi Umayya, was born into the prestigious Makhzumi tribe in Mecca. Little is known about her early life, but it is believed that she grew up in an environment characterized by piety, honor, and a strong sense of community. From a young age, Umm Salama demonstrated intelligence, resilience, and a keen interest in commerce, traits that would shape her future endeavors as a trader and supporter of Islam.

Role as a Trader:

Umm Salama emerged as a successful and respected trader, engaging in commerce across the Arabian Peninsula and beyond. Her business ventures involved the trading of goods such as textiles, spices, and precious metals, which brought her financial independence and recognition within

Meccan society. Despite her marriage to the Prophet Muhammad (ﷺ)(peace be upon him), Umm Salama continued her trading activities, demonstrating the compatibility of faith and worldly pursuits in Islam.

Marriage to the Prophet Muhammad:

Umm Salama's life took a significant turn when she married the Prophet Muhammad (ﷺ)(peace be upon him), becoming one of his esteemed wives. Despite the challenges and trials she faced throughout her life, Umm Salama remained steadfast in her faith and devotion to her husband, supporting him in his mission to spread the message of Islam. Her marriage to the Prophet Muhammad (ﷺ)exemplified the importance of mutual respect, love, and companionship in Islam.

Continuation of Trading Activities:

Despite her elevated status as the wife of the Prophet Muhammad, Umm Salama continued her trading activities, showcasing her independence and entrepreneurial spirit. She managed her business affairs with wisdom and foresight, using her wealth and resources to support her family and contribute to charitable causes. Umm Salama's ability to balance her roles as a wife, mother, and businesswoman serves as an inspiration for Muslim women seeking to pursue their passions and interests while upholding the teachings of Islam.

Legacy and Influence:

Umm Salama's legacy endures as a testament to the resilience, strength, and devotion of Muslim women throughout history. Her exemplary life serves as a source of inspiration for women seeking to navigate the complexities of life with faith, dignity, and perseverance. Umm Salama's commitment to her trading activities, even after embracing Islam and marrying the Prophet Muhammad, highlights the importance of economic empowerment and self-sufficiency for women in Islam.

Umm Salama's life exemplifies the harmonious integration of faith and worldly pursuits in Islam. As a successful trader and devoted wife of the Prophet Muhammad (ﷺ)(peace be upon him), she demonstrated the compatibility of entrepreneurship and piety, inspiring Muslim women to pursue their passions and interests while upholding the values of Islam. Umm Salama's legacy continues to resonate with believers around the world, serving as a timeless reminder of the important role that women play in shaping the course of history and advancing the cause of Islam.

Khadija bint Khawwab: The Supportive Sister of Umar ibn al-Khattab

Khadija bint Khawwab holds a significant place in Islamic history as the supportive sister of Umar ibn al-Khattab, one of the most prominent companions of the Prophet Muhammad (ﷺ)(peace be upon him) and the second caliph of Islam. Her steadfast support and encouragement of her brother, as well as her dedication to the early Muslim community, exemplify the vital role that family members played in the spread and consolidation of Islam during its formative years. This essay aims to explore the life, contributions, and legacy of Khadija bint Khawwab, shedding light on her relationship with Umar ibn al-Khattab and her impact on the Muslim community.

Early Life and Background:

Khadija bint Khawwab was born into the esteemed Banu Adi clan of the Quraysh tribe in Mecca. Little is known about her early life, but it is believed that she grew up in a household characterized by piety, honor, and a strong sense of familial bonds. As the sister of Umar ibn al-Khattab, Khadija witnessed firsthand the transformation of her brother from a staunch opponent of Islam to one of its most ardent supporters and leaders.

Support for Umar ibn al-Khattab:

Khadija bint Khawwab played a pivotal role in supporting her brother, Umar ibn al-Khattab, throughout his journey towards embracing Islam and his subsequent service to the Muslim community. Despite Umar's initial opposition to Islam and his persecution of its followers, Khadija remained steadfast in her support and encouragement of her brother, believing in his inherent goodness and potential for change. Her unwavering faith in Umar's character and her prayers for his guidance played a crucial role in his eventual acceptance of Islam.

Dedication to the Early Muslim Community:

Khadija bint Khawwab's commitment to the early Muslim community extended beyond her support for her brother. As a devout believer herself, she actively participated in the social and religious activities of the Muslim community, offering assistance and guidance to fellow believers. Her presence and encouragement provided strength and reassurance to those who faced persecution and hardship for their faith, fostering a sense of unity and solidarity among the early Muslims.

Legacy and Influence:

Khadija bint Khawwab's legacy as the supportive sister of Umar ibn al-Khattab endures as a testament to the transformative power of familial love and encouragement. Her unwavering faith in her brother's potential and her steadfast support of his endeavors played a crucial role in shaping the course of Islamic history. Khadija's example serves as a source of inspiration for believers, highlighting the importance of familial bonds and the power of encouragement in nurturing personal growth and spiritual development.

Khadija bint Khawwab's life exemplifies the profound impact that familial support and encouragement can have on individual transformation and societal change. As the supportive sister of Umar ibn al-Khattab, she played a vital role in his journey towards embracing Islam and his subsequent service to the Muslim community. Khadija's legacy serves as a timeless reminder of the importance of familial bonds and the power of encouragement in fostering personal growth, resilience, and devotion to faith.

Shifa bint Abdullah: The Enterprising Businesswoman and Benefactor of the Migration to Medina

Shifa bint Abdullah occupies a distinguished place in Islamic history as a skilled businesswoman and generous benefactor who played a pivotal role in financing the migration of the Prophet Muhammad (ﷺ)(peace be upon him) and his companions to Medina. Her entrepreneurial spirit, financial acumen, and commitment to supporting the early Muslim community exemplify the vital contributions of women to the spread and establishment of Islam. This essay aims to delve into the remarkable life, achievements, and legacy of Shifa bint Abdullah, shedding light on her background as a businesswoman, her philanthropic endeavors, and her enduring impact on the Muslim community.

Early Life and Background:

Shifa bint Abdullah was born into a respected family in Mecca, a city known for its commercial and religious significance. Little is known about her early life, but it is believed that she received a traditional upbringing characterized by piety, integrity, and a strong work ethic. From a young age, Shifa demonstrated intelligence, resilience, and a keen interest in commerce, traits that would shape her future endeavors as a businesswoman and supporter of Islam.

Role as a Businesswoman:

Shifa bint Abdullah emerged as a skilled and enterprising businesswoman, engaging in trade and commerce to support herself and her family. Her business ventures took her across the Arabian Peninsula, where she established lucrative commercial connections and traded in goods ranging from textiles to spices. Shifa's keen business acumen, integrity, and commitment to fair trade earned her a reputation as one of the most respected and influential merchants in Mecca.

Support for the Migration to Medina:

Shifa bint Abdullah's most notable contribution came in the form of her generous financial support for the migration (Hijrah) of the Prophet Muhammad (ﷺ)and his companions from Mecca to Medina. Recognizing the importance of establishing a safe haven for the Muslim community, Shifa generously donated her wealth to finance the migration, ensuring the safety and security of the Prophet and his followers. Her philanthropic gesture played a crucial role in the success of the migration and the establishment of Islam in Medina.

Impact on the Muslim Community:

The migration of the Prophet Muhammad (ﷺ)and his companions to Medina, made possible in part by Shifa bint Abdullah's generous contributions, had a profound impact on the early Muslim community and the course of Islamic history. It marked the beginning of a new chapter in the spread and consolidation of Islam, establishing Medina as a center of Islamic governance, scholarship, and community life. Shifa's support for the migration demonstrated the importance of financial contributions in advancing the cause of Islam and supporting the needs of the Muslim community.

Legacy and Influence:

Shifa bint Abdullah's legacy endures as a testament to the transformative power of philanthropy and the enduring impact of individual generosity on the development of Islamic institutions. Her selfless contributions to the migration to Medina exemplify the values of compassion, generosity, and devotion to God that are central to the teachings of Islam. Shifa's legacy continues to inspire Muslims around the world to follow her example of selfless giving and to contribute to the betterment of their communities through acts of charity and kindness.

Shifa bint Abdullah's life exemplifies the profound impact that individual initiative and generosity can have on the advancement of Islam and the welfare of the Muslim community. As a skilled businesswoman and generous benefactor, she played a vital role in supporting the migration of the Prophet Muhammad (ﷺ)and his companions to Medina, ensuring the safety and security of the Muslim community. Shifa's legacy serves as a timeless reminder of the importance of philanthropy and the power of individual contributions in advancing the cause of Islam and supporting the needs of the community.

Khawlah bint Hakim: Wealthy woman who offered her house as a meeting place for early Muslims.
Khawlah bint Hakim: The Generous Patroness of Early Islam

Khawlah bint Hakim occupies a revered position in Islamic history as a wealthy woman who played a crucial role in supporting the early Muslim community. Known for her generosity and hospitality, Khawlah opened her house as a meeting place for the Prophet Muhammad (ﷺ)(peace be upon him) and his companions, providing a safe haven for them to gather, worship, and strategize. This essay aims to explore the remarkable life, contributions, and legacy of Khawlah bint Hakim, shedding light on her background as a wealthy patroness, her pivotal role in early Islamic gatherings, and her enduring impact on the Muslim community.

Early Life and Background:

Khawlah bint Hakim was born into a noble and affluent family in pre-Islamic Arabia, where she enjoyed a privileged upbringing. Little is known about her early life, but it is believed that she received a comprehensive education and was raised with a strong sense of duty and honor. Khawlah's wealth and social standing afforded her the means to make significant contributions to her community and support noble causes.

Wealth and Generosity:

Khawlah bint Hakim emerged as a wealthy and philanthropic woman, using her resources to alleviate the suffering of the less fortunate and support the causes of justice and righteousness. Her generosity extended beyond material wealth, as she offered her time, energy, and influence to support the Prophet Muhammad (ﷺ)and his companions in their mission to spread the message of Islam. Khawlah's commitment to charitable giving and social justice earned her widespread admiration and respect among her contemporaries.

Role as a Patroness:

Khawlah bint Hakim played a pivotal role in early Islamic gatherings by offering her house as a meeting place for the Prophet Muhammad (ﷺ) and his companions. Recognizing the importance of providing a safe and welcoming space for the Muslim community to gather, Khawlah generously opened her doors to believers, allowing them to engage in worship, study, and consultation away from the prying eyes of their adversaries. Her house became a sanctuary for the early Muslims, fostering a sense of unity, solidarity, and mutual support among believers.

Support for the Prophet Muhammad:

Khawlah bint Hakim's support for the Prophet Muhammad (ﷺ) and his companions was unwavering, despite the challenges and persecution they faced from their adversaries. She provided both material and moral support to the Muslim community, offering her resources to fund their activities and her encouragement to bolster their spirits in times of adversity. Khawlah's commitment to the cause of Islam served as a source of inspiration and strength for the early Muslims, motivating them to persevere in the face of hardship and opposition.

Legacy and Influence:

Khawlah bint Hakim's legacy as a generous patroness of early Islam endures as a testament to the transformative power of philanthropy and hospitality. Her selfless contributions to the Muslim community, including her offering of her house as a meeting place for believers, exemplify the values of compassion, generosity, and solidarity that are central to the teachings of Islam. Khawlah's legacy continues to inspire Muslims around the world to follow her example of selfless giving and to support the needs of their communities through acts of charity, kindness, and hospitality.

:

Khawlah bint Hakim's life exemplifies the profound impact that individual generosity and hospitality can have on the development and growth of the Muslim community. As a wealthy patroness of early Islam, she played a crucial role in supporting the Prophet Muhammad (ﷺ) and his companions by offering her house as a meeting place for believers. Khawlah's legacy serves as a timeless reminder of the importance of philanthropy, hospitality, and solidarity in building strong and resilient communities based on the principles of compassion, justice, and righteousness.

Umm Sulaym: The Enterprising Woman of Faith Who Embraced Migration

Umm Sulaym stands as a prominent figure in Islamic history as a devout woman of faith and a resilient participant in the migration (Hijrah) to Medina alongside her husband. Known for her entrepreneurial spirit and unwavering commitment to Islam, Umm Sulaym's journey exemplifies the sacrifices made by early Muslim women in the pursuit of their faith and the establishment of a strong Muslim community. This essay aims to explore the remarkable life, achievements, and legacy of Umm Sulaym, shedding light on her background as a businesswoman, her role in the migration to Medina, and her enduring impact on the Muslim community.

Early Life and Background:

Umm Sulaym, also known as Umm Sulaym bint Milhan, was born into a respected family in Mecca, a city of great significance in pre-Islamic Arabia. Little is known about her early life, but she is remembered for her devout upbringing and strong sense of faith instilled by her parents. Umm Sulaym's upbringing laid the foundation for her later role as a committed Muslim and participant in the migration to Medina.

Role as a Businesswoman:

Umm Sulaym emerged as a skilled and enterprising businesswoman, engaging in trade and commerce to support herself and her family. Her business ventures took her across the Arabian Peninsula, where she established lucrative commercial connections and traded in goods ranging from textiles to foodstuffs. Umm Sulaym's entrepreneurial spirit and financial independence set her apart as a respected figure in Meccan society.

Participation in the Migration to Medina:

Umm Sulaym's most notable contribution came through her participation in the migration to Medina alongside her husband, Malik ibn Anas. Recognizing the importance of establishing a safe and thriving Muslim community, Umm Sulaym courageously embarked on the journey to Medina, leaving behind the comforts and familiarity of Mecca for the sake of her faith. Her decision to migrate exemplified her unwavering commitment to Islam and her willingness to sacrifice for the sake of Allah.

Support for the Prophet Muhammad:

Umm Sulaym's migration to Medina was not only an act of personal devotion but also a demonstration of her support for the Prophet Muhammad (ﷺ) and his mission. By joining the Prophet and his companions in their migration, Umm Sulaym contributed to the establishment of a strong Muslim community in Medina, where Islam could flourish and spread freely. Her presence and participation served as a source of encouragement and inspiration for fellow believers, strengthening their resolve in the face of adversity.

Legacy and Influence:

Umm Sulaym's legacy as a devout woman of faith and a resilient participant in the migration to Medina endures as a testament to the sacrifices made by early Muslim women in the cause of Islam. Her unwavering commitment to her faith and her willingness to forsake the comforts of home for the sake of Allah serve as a timeless example for Muslims around the world. Umm Sulaym's story inspires believers to emulate her courage, devotion, and selflessness in their own lives, striving to uphold the teachings of Islam in all aspects of their existence.

Umm Sulaym's life exemplifies the courage, faith, and resilience of early Muslim women who played a crucial role in the establishment and spread of Islam. As a businesswoman who participated in the migration to Medina, she demonstrated her unwavering commitment to her faith and her willingness to sacrifice for the sake of Allah. Umm Sulaym's legacy serves as a timeless reminder of the importance of steadfastness, devotion, and sacrifice in the pursuit of righteousness and the establishment of a strong and vibrant Muslim community.

Fatima bint Khayyat: Skilled tailor and businesswoman who supported her family and the Muslim community.

Fatima bint Khayyat: The Talented Tailor and Supportive Businesswoman

Fatima bint Khayyat holds a revered place in Islamic history as a skilled tailor and enterprising businesswoman who supported her family and the Muslim community during the early years of Islam. Known for her craftsmanship, entrepreneurial spirit, and unwavering commitment to Islam, Fatima's story exemplifies the vital contributions of women to the economic and social fabric of society. This essay aims to explore the remarkable life, achievements, and legacy of Fatima bint Khayyat, shedding light on her background as a tailor, her role as a businesswoman, and her enduring impact on the Muslim community.

Early Life and Background:

Fatima bint Khayyat was born into a modest family in Mecca, a city known for its bustling markets and diverse trades. From a young age, Fatima demonstrated a natural talent for tailoring and sewing, skills that she would later cultivate into a successful business. Despite the challenges of her upbringing, Fatima's determination and perseverance set her on a path towards financial independence and entrepreneurial success.

Role as a Tailor:

Fatima bint Khayyat emerged as a skilled and sought-after tailor, renowned for her craftsmanship and attention to detail. Her talents in sewing and garment-making earned her a loyal clientele among the residents of Mecca, who sought her services for their clothing and textile needs. Fatima's dedication to her craft and commitment to quality set her apart as a respected figure in the local tailoring industry.

Entrepreneurial Spirit:

In addition to her skills as a tailor, Fatima bint Khayyat possessed a strong entrepreneurial spirit, which she utilized to support her family and contribute to the welfare of the Muslim community. Recognizing the demand for her services, Fatima expanded her business operations, establishing her own workshop and employing other women to assist her in fulfilling orders. Her enterprising endeavors not only provided a source of income for her family but also created employment opportunities for other women in the community.

Support for the Muslim Community:

Fatima bint Khayyat's contributions extended beyond her business activities to encompass her support for the Muslim community during the early years of Islam. Recognizing the importance of solidarity and mutual support, Fatima generously offered her services and resources to assist her fellow believers in times of need. Whether through providing clothing for the less fortunate or offering financial assistance to those in distress, Fatima demonstrated her commitment to the welfare of the Muslim community and the principles of charity and compassion.

Legacy and Influence:

Fatima bint Khayyat's legacy as a skilled tailor and supportive businesswoman endures as a testament to the resilience, ingenuity, and generosity of women in Islam. Her entrepreneurial spirit and commitment to excellence serve as a source of inspiration for Muslim women seeking to pursue their passions and contribute to the betterment of their communities. Fatima's story highlights the importance of economic empowerment and self-sufficiency for women in Islam, as well as the significant role that women played in the economic and social development of early Muslim societies.

Fatima bint Khayyat's life exemplifies the transformative power of talent, entrepreneurship, and generosity in shaping the course of history and advancing the cause of Islam. As a skilled tailor and supportive businesswoman, she made significant contributions to her family and the Muslim community, demonstrating the invaluable role that women play in the economic and social fabric of society. Fatima's legacy continues to inspire believers around the world to harness their talents and resources for the greater good, striving to uphold the principles of Islam in all aspects of their lives.

Zaynab bint Jahsh: Prophet Muhammad's (PBUH) cousin and businesswoman who migrated to Medina.

Zaynab bint Jahsh: The Resilient Businesswoman and Faithful Migrant to Medina

Zaynab bint Jahsh occupies a significant place in Islamic history as the cousin of Prophet Muhammad (ﷺ)(peace be upon him) and a pioneering businesswoman who played a pivotal role in the early Muslim community. Known for her resilience, faith, and entrepreneurial spirit, Zaynab's journey from Mecca to Medina exemplifies the sacrifices made by early Muslims in the pursuit of their faith and the establishment of a strong Muslim community. This essay aims to explore the remarkable life, achievements, and legacy of Zaynab bint Jahsh, shedding light on her background as a businesswoman, her migration to Medina, and her enduring impact on the Muslim community.

Early Life and Background:

Zaynab bint Jahsh was born into the noble and prestigious Banu Hashim clan of the Quraysh tribe in Mecca. As a cousin of the Prophet Muhammad, Zaynab grew up in an environment steeped in the traditions of her noble lineage and the teachings of Islam. From a young age, she demonstrated intelligence, resilience, and a keen interest in commerce, traits that would shape her future endeavors as a businesswoman and supporter of Islam.

Role as a Businesswoman:

Zaynab bint Jahsh emerged as a skilled and enterprising businesswoman, engaging in trade and commerce to support herself and her family. Her business ventures took her across the Arabian Peninsula, where she established lucrative commercial connections and traded in goods ranging from textiles to spices. Zaynab's entrepreneurial spirit, integrity, and commitment to fair trade earned her a reputation as one of the most respected and influential merchants in Mecca.

Migration to Medina:

Zaynab bint Jahsh's life took a significant turn with the migration (Hijrah) of the Prophet Muhammad (ﷺ)and his companions to Medina. Recognizing the importance of establishing a safe haven for the Muslim community, Zaynab courageously embarked on the journey to Medina alongside her husband, Zayd ibn Harithah. Their migration marked a new chapter in the history of Islam, as the Muslim community found refuge and support in the city of Medina, away from the persecution of their adversaries in Mecca.

Support for the Prophet Muhammad:

Zaynab bint Jahsh's migration to Medina was not only an act of personal devotion but also a demonstration of her support for the Prophet Muhammad (ﷺ)and his mission. By joining the Prophet and his companions in their migration, Zaynab contributed to the establishment of a strong Muslim community in Medina, where Islam could flourish and spread freely. Her presence and participation served as a source of encouragement and inspiration for fellow believers, strengthening their resolve in the face of adversity.

Legacy and Influence:

Zaynab bint Jahsh's legacy as a resilient businesswoman and faithful migrant to Medina endures as a testament to the sacrifices made by early Muslims in the cause of Islam. Her unwavering commitment to her faith, her entrepreneurial spirit, and her willingness to sacrifice for the sake of Allah serve as timeless examples for Muslims around the world. Zaynab's story inspires believers to emulate her courage, devotion, and selflessness in their own lives, striving to uphold the teachings of Islam in all aspects of their existence.

Zaynab bint Jahsh's life exemplifies the resilience, faith, and entrepreneurial spirit of early Muslim women who played a crucial role in the establishment and spread of Islam. As a businesswoman who migrated to Medina, she demonstrated her unwavering commitment to her faith and her willingness to sacrifice for the sake of Allah. Zaynab's legacy serves as a timeless reminder of the importance of steadfastness, devotion, and sacrifice in the pursuit of righteousness and the establishment of a strong and vibrant Muslim community.

Lessons from the Sahaba: Cultivating Ethical Entrepreneurship in Today's World

The world of business today faces numerous challenges, from navigating turbulent economies to confronting ethical dilemmas. While the context of early Islamic trade differs vastly from our modern landscape, the wisdom of the Sahaba, Prophet Muhammad's (PBUH) companions, still offers valuable lessons for aspiring entrepreneurs seeking to navigate the complexities of the modern business world with integrity and purpose.

Beyond Profit: Redefining Success with Ethical Values

For the Sahaba, trade wasn't solely about maximizing profits. Their approach was deeply rooted in Islamic principles, prioritizing fairness, honesty, and social responsibility. This translates into several key lessons for modern entrepreneurs:

Integrity Above All: Like the Sahaba who earned reputations for unwavering honesty, modern entrepreneurs must commit to ethical conduct, even when faced with tempting shortcuts or opportunities for deceit. Building trust with customers, partners, and employees forms the bedrock of sustainable success.

Just Practices, Just Profits: Avoiding exploitative practices like usury and prioritizing fair pricing, like the Sahaba did, promotes social justice and ensures prosperity is shared across communities. This doesn't preclude profitability, but it redefines success beyond mere financial gain.

Social Responsibility as a Core Value: Philanthropy wasn't an afterthought for the Sahaba; it was embedded in their business practices. Modern entrepreneurs can emulate this by integrating social responsibility initiatives into their core operations, contributing to positive social change and fostering meaningful community connections.

Innovation with Morality: Balancing Progress with Values

The Sahaba weren't just ethical; they were innovative. They developed the "hawala" system for secure cross-border transactions, demonstrating their adaptability and problem-solving skills. This translates into lessons for modern entrepreneurs:

Ethical Innovation: Technology offers vast opportunities for progress, but it must be harnessed responsibly. Entrepreneurs must consider the ethical implications of new technologies and ensure they align with their values, prioritizing data privacy, responsible AI development, and fair labor practices in the digital age.

Sustainability Beyond Profits: The Sahaba understood the long-term impact of their actions. Modern entrepreneurs can learn from their approach by integrating sustainability practices into their businesses, considering the environmental and social impact of their operations and seeking solutions that promote future generations' well-being.

Adapting to Change with Integrity: Just as the Sahaba navigated a dynamic trading environment, today's entrepreneurs face an ever-changing landscape. Embracing ethical principles as core values allows for flexible adaptation while maintaining trust and integrity, even amidst disruption and shifting market trends.

Building Trust and Community: The Power of Transparency and Collaboration

The Sahaba were known for their openness and collaborative spirit. They shared knowledge, resolved disputes fairly, and built trust with diverse communities. This translates into lessons for modern entrepreneurs:

Transparency Builds Trust: In an age of information overload, transparency is more critical than ever. Open communication with stakeholders, clear disclosure of practices, and honest marketing foster trust and loyalty in customers, partners, and employees.

Collaboration for Social Good: The Sahaba understood the power of collective action. Modern entrepreneurs can harness the power of collaboration to tackle social challenges, partnering with NGOs, social enterprises, and other businesses to drive positive change in their communities.

Fostering Inclusive Workplaces: Recognizing the value of diversity, the Sahaba embraced collaboration with individuals from various backgrounds. Modern entrepreneurs can cultivate inclusive workplaces that empower diverse talents and create an environment where everyone feels valued and respected.

Beyond Imitation: Embracing the Spirit of the Sahaba

It's important to acknowledge that simply mimicking the practices of the Sahaba wouldn't translate directly into our modern context. The key lies in understanding the underlying principles and values that guided their actions and applying them to the challenges and opportunities we face today.

This necessitates critical reflection on ethical dilemmas, seeking guidance from Islamic scholarly interpretations, and engaging in open dialogue with diverse stakeholders. By combining timeless values with contemporary knowledge and innovation, modern entrepreneurs can pave the way for a more ethical and sustainable business landscape.

Exploring Specific Examples: Learning from the Lives of Prominent Entrepreneurs

Further exploration of the lives and business practices of specific Sahaba like Khadija bint Khuwaylid, a successful merchant, and Abd al-Rahman ibn Awf, known for his financial management skills, can offer concrete examples of applying these principles in real-world scenarios. Studying their approaches to negotiation, risk management, and building community relationships can provide valuable insights for modern entrepreneurs.

The Journey of Ethical Entrepreneurship: A Continuous Learning Process

Incorporating the wisdom of the Sahaba into one's business journey requires ongoing learning and reflection. Engaging with contemporary scholars, participating in workshops and discussions on Islamic business ethics, and actively seeking feedback from diverse stakeholders can guide entrepreneurs in navigating complex situations and making ethical choices.

Ultimately, embracing the spirit of the Sahaba offers

Dua for Increased Wealth:

Seeking lawful sustenance through trade is encouraged. The Prophet (peace be upon him) said:

عَنْ صَخْرٍ الْغَامِدِيّ قَالَ قَالَ رَسُولُ اللّهِ صَلّى اللّهُ عَلَيْهِ وَسَلّمَ اللّهُمّ بَارِكْ لأُمّتِي فِي بُكُورِهَا

حَدّثَنَا أَحْمَدُ بْنُ سِنَانٍ، حَدّثَنَا كَثِيرُ بْنُ هِشَامٍ، حَدّثَنَا كُلْثُومُ بْنُ جَوْشَنٍ الْقُشَيْرِيُّ، عَنْ أَيّوبَ، عَنْ نَافِعٍ، عَنِ ابْنِ عُمَرَ، قَالَ: قَالَ رَسُولُ اللّهِ صَلّى اللّهُ عَلَيْهِ وَسَلّمَ: التّاجِرُ الأَمِينُ الصّدّوقُ الْمُسْلِمُ مَعَ الشّهَدَاءِ يَوْمَ الْقِيَامَةِ .

It was narrated from Ibn 'Umar that the Messenger of Allah (ﷺ) said:'The trustworthy, honest Muslim merchant will be with the martyrs on the Day of Resurrection. (Sunan Ibn Majah, 2139) Sahih Bukhari, Book 34:

Feelings

It's understandable to feel frustrated and perplexed by the prevalence of job dependence among Muslims today, especially when considering the entrepreneurial spirit and self-sufficiency demonstrated by the Sahaba. In a world abundant with technological advancements and opportunities, it's disheartening to see many of us still tethered to traditional employment structures.

As Muslims, we are called upon to follow the path of Allah and emulate the teachings of the Prophet Muhammad, peace be upon him. This includes embodying the entrepreneurial spirit and self-reliance exemplified by the Sahaba, who balanced their worldly pursuits with devotion to Allah. Their commitment to business and trade was not separate from their faith; rather, it was an extension of their dedication to serving their community and upholding Islamic principles.

So why are many of us hesitant to pursue entrepreneurship and business ventures despite the resources and opportunities available to us? Perhaps it's a combination of factors, including fear of failure, lack of confidence, and societal pressure to conform to conventional career paths. Additionally, the comfort and stability offered by traditional employment may deter some from taking the risk of starting their own businesses.

However, it's crucial to recognize that entrepreneurship and business ownership are not only avenues for financial success but also opportunities for personal growth, self-discovery, and service to others. By harnessing the power of technology and innovation, we have the potential to create businesses that not only thrive in the marketplace but also contribute positively to society and uphold Islamic values.

As Muslims, we should strive to break free from the cycle of job dependence and cultivate an entrepreneurial mindset rooted in faith, perseverance, and resilience. This may require stepping out of our comfort zones, seeking mentorship and guidance, and embracing failure as a learning opportunity on the path to success.

Ultimately, by aligning our business endeavors with the teachings of Islam and the examples set by the Prophet Muhammad (ﷺ)and the Sahaba, we can fulfill our duty to Allah while also realizing our potential as enterprising individuals. Let's harness the blessings of technology and innovation to create businesses that not only enrich our lives but also contribute to the betterment of our communities and the world at large.